D1476908

Jeans of the Old West
A History

MICHAEL A. HARRIS

Schiffer Publishing Ltd

4880 Lower Valley Road, Atglen, PA 19310

Other Schiffer Books on Related Subjects:
Denim: An American Story. David Little. ISBN: 9780764326868.
  $29.95
Mining in the Old West. Sandor Demlinger. ISBN: 0764323547.
  $29.95
The West that Was. John Eggen. ISBN: 0887403301. $29.95

Library of Congress Control Number: 2010925680

Designed by John P. Cheek
Cover design by Bruce Waters
Type set in Americana XBd BT/New Baskerville BT

ISBN: 978-0-7643-3500-6
Printed in China

Schiffer Books are available at special discounts for bulk
purchases for sales promotions or premiums. Special edi-
tions, including personalized covers, corporate imprints,
and excerpts can be created in large quantities for special
needs. For more information contact the publisher:

Published by Schiffer Publishing Ltd.
4880 Lower Valley Road
Atglen, PA 19310
Phone: (610) 593-1777; Fax: (610) 593-2002
E-mail: Info@schifferbooks.com

For the largest selection of fine reference books on this
and related subjects, please visit our web site at
www.schifferbooks.com
We are always looking for people to write books on new
and related subjects. If you have an idea for a book please
contact us at the above address.

This book may be purchased from the publisher.
Include $5.00 for shipping.
Please try your bookstore first.
You may write for a free catalog.

In Europe, Schiffer books are distributed by
Bushwood Books
6 Marksbury Ave.
Kew Gardens
Surrey TW9 4JF England
Phone: 44 (0) 20 8392 8585; Fax: 44 (0) 20 8392 9876
E-mail: info@bushwoodbooks.co.uk
Website: www.bushwoodbooks.co.uk

Contents

Foreword

When I initially considered writing this book, I had a fairly simple purpose in mind. I wanted to create a collector's guide for others who share my interest in the clothing worn by people who lived and worked in the American West during the middle of the nineteenth century. Specifically, I planned to focus on the work pants we know as jeans, because they are widely appreciated and collected by a growing community of enthusiasts (of whom I am one). However, as the work progressed, I came to recognize that the story of the invention and subsequent refinement of the denim work pants is part of a larger narrative. While I have included many photographs and much technical information that will be of interest to the collector, I also have attempted to describe how these artifacts fit into a larger story about the people and events that played a role in their creation.

It is surprisingly difficult to obtain accurate information about old jeans, considering that they were first manufactured commercially in a major American city only about 150 years ago. Relatively speaking, that wasn't so long ago. If one were investigating the history of some other, equally familiar item from that period (such as, say, Colt revolvers), most of the relevant information could be found in museums and records of the era, of which there are many. However, these pants were made in San Francisco, a city that was ravaged by fire several times since 1850. The records of their manufacture perished along with much of the city and many of its inhabitants. In addition, it must be remembered that early jeans were created and produced in what was still the frontier of North America, far from the manufacturing centers on the East Coast.

Because of the circumstances cited above, the quest for information about historic jeans involves a great deal of time spent searching for clues. In the absence of written documentation, much of the information about old jeans comes from the jeans themselves – from specimens that have survived. I apologize in advance for the tattered condition of many of the pieces of the old jeans used as examples in the illustrations for this book. Most of the pants in these photographs are held in private collections, including my own. Considering the limited production runs for some of these jeans, and the difficult conditions under which they were used, the fact that any examples remain is a testament to the quality of their design and construction. I enjoy examining the wear, stains, and tears on the jeans. They tell a story that has not yet been told. The marks of use on these jeans tell me as much about the lives of the men who wore them as books do: the candle wax that drips on the legs of a miner working hundreds of feet down in a mineshaft, the acid from processing metals at a mill, and the rips from the repetitive use of tools. I am accustomed to seeing jeans in this condition and to me it is as authentic as it comes. Truly, the birth place and development of denim as we know it happened because of the extreme conditions found in the work places of the Old West, where the strength of the pants were pushed to their limit and beyond. In these places these jeans were not worn as in the malls of today; the journey they took is a fascinating one that never ceases to give me clues, and every different pair has a story to tell about the Old West.

There are various reasons why people are fascinated by old jeans. For some, they are an accessible connection to a romanticized period of American history, easily recognized and appreciated because the descendants of those original designs are still popular today. The photos and information in this book are evidence that many of the styling features incorporated into modern "designer" jeans originated in the workshops of nineteenth century craftsmen seeking ways to make improved work pants. Others are interested in old jeans as part of a general interest in American antiquities. Viewed as cultural artifacts, old jeans can tell us much about the way people lived and worked in the boomtowns of the Old West. What may not be so obvious is that these pants represent the birth of an industry; at least two modern-day clothing manufacturers started out making work clothes in San Francisco during the 1870s.

At present there is little to be found on the study of non-riveted jeans dating from the seventeen year period that *Levi Strauss & Co.* held the patent on rivets. The designs that companies came up with to strengthen the stress points of the pants were amazing, beautiful, but also functional. Those jeans functioned under conditions we can hardly imagine today. When the patent expired on rivets in 1890, so did most of the non-riveted designs. I feel lucky to be able to bring these little known and little understood designs to light and I hope the reader grows to appreciate these garments as much as I do. A word about the terms used in this book: In the late 1800s, the word "overalls" was used to describe waist work pants made of heavy material. The modern usage of the term "overalls" generally is reserved for pants with a part covering the chest. In this book, I use the old meaning of the term "overalls" and use the term "bib-overalls" for the modern meaning. Generally, I use the words "jeans," "work pants," and "overalls," synonymously.

I wish to thank the many people who helped me write this book and who helped me over the past several years in gathering information about jeans of the Old West. Most importantly, I thank my wife, Charla Harris, for her long hours in editing the text, taking pictures, editing all of the graphics, and for her passion for the subject matter that helped in the

long process of gathering the materials for this book. I also thank my father-in-law, Russ Miller, for his knowledge of the West, his enormous research efforts spent in libraries and archives, and his editing skills, without which I could not have compiled the book; my uncle-in-law, Dan Gaither, for extensively editing the book, and my mother-in-law, Carole Miller, for gathering genealogical information on all of the people mentioned in the book. There were several others who contributed material for the book: a special thanks to Ralph Tharpe, Director of Technical Design at Cone Denim, LLC, for sharing his expertise of denim manufacturing; Hitoshi Yamada, for letting me use his extensive collection; Mike Hodis, of the Rising Sun & Co., for his expertise and collection; Brit Eaton at www.carpedenim.com for letting me use pictures of his collection; Cholatee "Tee" Komol, Glenn Mariconda, Gordon Muir, and the "Inyo Kid." Other people who contributed information and ideas were: Madeline Harmon of Chuck's Vintage, Douglas and Hampus Luhanko of Blue Highway, Viktor Fredback, and Janet and Paul Andrews.

The gathering of information in libraries and archives could not have been done without the assistance of Lara Michels, Associate Archivist and Librarian at the Judah L Magnes Museum; Tami Suzuki, Librarian at the San Francisco Public Library; and Kathryn Totton, Photograph Curator, University of Nevada, Reno Libraries. Lastly, I would like to thank my stepfather, Paul Andrews, for his companionship on many of the long journeys.

— Michael Allen Harris

Introduction

California's early history was one of incessant political and cultural change; eight flags had flown over California lands, and California had even been a republic for a brief period, before the Stars and Stripes were raised on July 9 of 1846. Separated from the political power centers on the East Coast by vast, unsettled territory, California was home to a diverse, energetic population that prospered in isolation. That changed in dramatic fashion, however, in January of 1848, when gold was discovered at Sutter's Mill, and the biggest rush of people and materials the Nation had yet seen headed for California. Although the initial surge of gold-seekers had slowed by the time California was admitted to the Union as the thirty-first state on September 9, 1850, the State would never resume its isolated status. By then, California had become the primary destination for the people and commodities fueling the expansive growth in the West. With its magnificent seaport and proximity to the gold and silver fields in the deserts and mountains, San Francisco was ideally situated as a mercantile center for the region.

Thousands of ships bringing men and supplies to the Gold Rush of 1848 docked in the harbor at San Francisco. Yankee Clippers like the *Black Hawk*, pictured here moored at San Francisco, were the most common type of trade ship of the time (Photo courtesy of San Francisco Public Library, Historical Photograph Collection).

Dry goods, canned goods, and mining paraphernalia was bought off the boats by merchants who saw that it quickly got into the hands of the gold seekers. One hundred miles to the east, tens of thousands of avid prospectors crawled over each gully and ridge of the Sierra Nevada foothills. People came from all over the world to get rich in California; in China, California is still referred to as "The Mountain of Gold." Although many found nothing, others saw their dreams of wealth become reality. Gold was found in huge quantities, and quickly became the currency of California. At $16 an ounce, a pinch of gold dust (as much as a wet thumb and forefinger could pick up) was reckoned to be a dollar's worth. (Kahn, 2002, p. 384).

The frenzied movement of supplies from the ships to the merchants, and on to the mining camps, was driven by the enormous wealth that people were getting for their efforts. All manner of materials found value. A young lad, newly arrived from New York by ship via Panama, was unloading his wares, when a man quickly approached him and asked "How much do you want for that big box?" "One hundred and fifty dollars," was the lad's answer. "I'll give you $100." The deal was made without the buyer even asking what was in it. The man carefully opened the large crate (it was seven feet tall) revealing a wagon and said, "Stranger, you may keep the wagon, for I only want the box." (Narell, 1981, p. 35).

In the foothill mining camps that seemingly appeared overnight, the conditions were primitive at best. A store was often a small plot of ground walled by piled brush with items for sale hanging from branches. None of this mattered, however, as supplies were sold quickly. Miners and prospectors often would come into the mining camps on weekends to buy new outfittings, especially clothing, and discard the old ones on the store floor (Kahn, 2002, p. 321). Literally, time was money.

Opposite page:
San Francisco's Battery Street in 1856. Large brick and stone buildings already line the street where Levi Strauss & Co. and many of its competitors would be headquartered in the 1860s. (courtesy of San Francisco Public Library, Historical Photograph Collection.)

The enormous influx of people seeking to become rich from the goldfields, coupled with the surge of wealth from the gold being found, brought big changes to the region. These changes were nowhere more evident than in San Francisco; someone who had seen the City in its infancy in 1849 would return to find a major metropolis in 1870—the tenth largest city in the U.S. (Kahn, 2002, p. 52). In an ominous portent of things to come, the crude town that existed in 1849 had been swept away by fire six times by the middle of 1851 (Narell, 1981, p. 36). But business hardly slowed long enough to carry away the burnt debris. The large four-story brick and stone churches, temples, mansions, and business buildings that rose from the ashes of incinerated shanties made an impressive sight. No longer an outpost in the wilderness, San Francisco had by 1851 established itself as a modern city.

The Early Clothing Industry of San Francisco

In spite of its abundant material wealth and social energy, San Francisco remained at mid-century largely a terminal for the transshipment of goods made elsewhere. Ships continued to arrive every day, carrying goods bound for the Mother Lode area. In those early days, there was little manufacturing in San Francisco. The city's stores and warehouses were stocked primarily with items that could be shipped by Yankee Clippers around the Horn of South America. Goods found their way from the ships to consumers through a variety of business arrangements. Some merchants ordered goods directly from suppliers in the East, while others bought goods off the ships, as they needed them to stock their shelves. A large group of "commission merchants" ran businesses buying goods off the ships and reselling them by auction or directly to wholesalers in the city.

However, despite of the frenetic efforts of the shipping and mercantile companies, there were some requirements that could not be met by suppliers on the other side of the continent. Chief among these was the rapidly growing need for sturdy work clothes that fit, and for the mending of damaged clothes. Accordingly, a large and prosperous tailoring industry developed in the city. Anyone with needles and thread could start a thriving business—the man who bought the large crate was a shoemaker looking for a place to set up shop. Although the city lacked the infrastructure to support most kinds of industrial manufacturing, conditions would allow the manufacture of clothing to fill the needs of the men seeking their fortunes in the hills and deserts.

The heart of the San Francisco clothing district in 1870. The east side of Sansom Street between Bush and Pine streets. (courtesy of San Francisco Public Library, Historical Photograph Collection.)

Battery Street in 1880. (courtesy of San Francisco Public Library, Historical Photograph Collection.)

As soon as the words "gold in California" spread around the world, a constant stream of immigrants began arriving in San Francisco. Many of them came from Eastern Europe, and a great many of those were young Jewish men. This was no happy coincidence; rather, it was the result of unfortunate events abroad that produced an exodus of young Jewish men from Germany and Prussia in the 1840s and 1850s. Not only had the Jewish population of those areas been politically oppressed, the military-aged men were subject to conscription, often by nighttime raids (Kahn, 2002, p. 128). The result was that, even before the discovery of gold in California, young Jewish men were arriving in the United States, looking for opportunities. In time, some of these men would become the proprietors of San Francisco's leading clothing and dry goods firms, and would go on to create a garment industry on the West Coast. Along the way, they would provide their adopted nation with one of its most enduring cultural icons: denim jeans.

Some did try their hand at prospecting for gold in the mining camps; but most Eastern European Jewish men sought their fortunes as merchants in San Fran-

cisco and the Gold Rush supply towns (Kahn, 2002, p. 385). The penchant for Eastern European Jewish immigrants to gravitate to the dry-goods business, including clothing and "gents' furnishing goods," can be explained by the historical treatment of Jews in Europe. They had been given very limited access to employment opportunities in their homelands, and the clothing industry was one of the few livelihoods in which they could become prosperous. For instance, a mid-century Jewish immigrant from the town of Aix la Chapelle, in what was then Prussia, noted that the population of 60,000 to 70,000 was mostly in the business of manufacturing broadcloth and fine cloths (Kahn, 2002, p. 442).

The speed and skill with which these new immigrants applied their knowledge to develop the clothing industry in San Francisco during this period is noteworthy. A visitor to the San Francisco quarter taken over by the textile and ready-made clothes businesses in 1856 described the district as "...an endless series of signs, for the most part displaying in shiny gold letters Jewish names, almost all of them deriving from Jewish families of Europe (Kahn, 2002, p. 87)."

From the first days of the Gold Rush in 1848, to at least the mid-1860s, clothing was shipped continually from the East Coast to San Francisco. But, as cheap labor became available, some merchants began manufacturing clothes locally. The cheap labor was a result of the playing out of the major surface gold fields that had been easy pickings for individual miners. Where once a man could make a living (and sometimes a fortune) on an eight-by-sixteen-foot claim (Rochlin & Rochlin, 2000, p. 30), by the end of 1860 only large companies of men working giant hydraulic monitors were to be seen. As the opportunities became fewer, many prospectors wandered back to San Francisco seeking work or a way home. These job seekers joined the shiploads of Chinese immigrants who arrived each day looking for work in the city. China was a common destination for trade ships on the West Coast, sometimes hauling such mundane cargo as laundry (it being so much cheaper to have it washed there than in San Francisco – and, they starched it!). A common response to the question of where a miner's Sunday shirt was would be "It's on a slow boat to China."

With slim pickings in the gold fields, most of the Chinese immigrants stayed in San Francisco, and many found employment in the clothing manufacturing industry (Glanz, 1954, p. 221 and Kahn, 2002, p. 460). They mostly made dress clothes, which had to be made to order for fit; it is assumed that work pantaloons (pants) were still made back East.

For the reasons noted above, it is somewhat difficult to state with certainty the extent to which locally-produced work pants had entered the San Francisco market prior to 1860. However, a careful examination of the few records (especially photographic) of the era may provide some useful insights. For example, consider the way that men held up their pants. The typical pantaloons of 1860 had no belt loops; only a small cinch strap in the back could be used for waist-size adjustment. A split in the middle back of the waistband also gave extra room. But, if necessary, suspenders could be worn—waistline buttons being provided for them on most pants. The lack of suspenders shown being worn in photos of workingmen of the times indicates there were large quantities of various sizes available. However, when one considers that in California the bulk of these garments were brought in by ship, one gets a sense of the enormity of the enterprise required to supply the men who worked the gold fields.

The problem of supply was made worse by the extreme challenges posed by working conditions in the West. Standard work pants wore out rapidly under the heavy labor of the mines and mills. Tailors could make some repairs, but usually worn out work pants were discarded. Undoubtedly, this exacerbated the problem of meeting the demand for work pants on the West Coast by shipping them in. However, the same conditions that posed challenges for mercantile suppliers created opportunities for local entrepreneurs.

The Marsac Silver Mill in Nevada in 1885. These mills, all over Nevada, bought large quantities of work pants. (courtesy of Special Collections Department, University of Nevada, Reno Library.)

THE INVENTORS AND MANUFACTURERS OF STRENGTHENED WORK PANTS

With the decline of the California gold mines in the late 1850s came the discovery of silver in Nevada—the Comstock Lode at Virginia City in 1858 being by far the biggest strike (Rochlin & Rochlin, 2000, p. 31). Gold seekers that had missed finding their fortunes in California, accompanied by a swelling horde of latecomers, filled mining boomtowns all over Nevada. San Francisco goods had a new place to go, and wagon trains loaded with supplies headed east on new roads. A few intrepid tailors followed to be close to the men who needed their skills. Jacob W. Davis was one of them (Cray, 1978, p. 17).

Miners gathered for a photograph during a shift change at the Eureka Silver Mine in Eureka, Nevada—about 1870.
(courtesy of Special Collections Department, University of Nevada, Reno Library.)

Working out of a shop in Reno, Jacob Davis custom made work pants and other hand-sewn items for men who were too big to wear the available ready-mades being wagonned out from San Francisco. Although he had no way of knowing it at the time, Jacob made clothing history one day in his primitive workshop, when the idea came to him to use the same rivets for work pants that he had been using for making horse blankets (Cray, 1978, p. 18). His customers immediately saw the value of his innovation. They started telling others, and soon he was getting more orders than he could fill. Imitation being the sincerest form of flattery, other tailors in town shortly began to eye his new, riveted pantaloons. However, Jacob Davis evidently was as canny a businessman as he was a craftsman and innovator. He sensed that he was on to something big, and he took action to capitalize on the opportunity.

Knowing that he didn't have the time to fill all of the orders, or the money to protect his invention, he turned to Levi Strauss, with whom he already had a working relationship. Levi Strauss' company in San Francisco had been supplying Jacob Davis with denim cloth and other materials for some time, and Jacob knew Levi well enough to send a personal letter asking for his assistance (Cray, 1978, p. 20 & 21). Levi responded by offering Jacob a job as foreman overseeing the manufacturing of the new riveted pants, and full backing for a patent. On May 20, 1873, the patent for riveted pantaloons was granted by the U.S. Patent Office and *Levi Strauss & Co.* began selling the improved pants for more than other pants. But, the new pants were popular and outsold the others. Davis' idea was taking hold, and his decision to team up with Levi Strauss and patent his design ensured that riveted jeans would dominate the market for years to come.

The other clothing merchants in San Francisco on Battery and Sansome streets found their pants no longer selling well in the mining towns of Nevada. To add to their frustration, they would have to wait seventeen years until the patent ran out before they too could make riveted pants. So, to compete with Levi Strauss & Co., the other merchants had to come up with inventions of their own—other ways to strengthen work pants. Riveting was the most elegant solution to the problem of tearing pocket corners; but, several of Levi's competitors did introduce other designs, some of which could be quickly and cheaply made. The new pants designs would have had to be manufactured in San Francisco; it would have taken too long to set up the manufacturing on the East Coast and ship them to California.

To fully appreciate the challenges faced by the makers of work pants within the competitive environment of San Francisco during the latter part of the nineteenth century, one must consider the nature of the actual item they were producing, and its intended consumers. The fact is that jeans are really pretty simple garments. There are only a few features that may be altered in order to improve on the basic design. Moreover, the miners and mill workers for whom these pants were being made were concerned primarily in durability and comfort, not style. Generally speaking, *strength* became the measure of *value*. As always, price mattered; however, because men working in remote places where it was often not possible to replace worn-out items quickly used the pants, durability took on added importance. It follows, then, that people who wanted to challenge Levi Strauss for a bigger share of the jeans market focused on ways to make their pants stronger without risking a lawsuit for patent infringement.

Because jeans are such simple garments, the study of jeans involves careful attention to the few details that separate various designs. Often, the architecture of something as elemental as a watch pocket or waistband is sufficient to distinguish pants made in one year from those made the following year. Refinements of these basic features represent the efforts of creative, energetic men engaged in a competition for market share in a fledgling American industry. The text and illustrations in this book are presented in an effort to provide both the collector and casual reader with the information needed to recognize and appreciate these nuances.

Jacob Greenebaum was the first to meet the challenge. He was already a principal partner of *Greenebaum Brothers*, a San Francisco dealer in gents' furnishing goods. His solution was simple, cheap, and could be applied to pants already made: a leather triangle sewn over the pocket corners.

David Neustadter was next. A family member, though only a salesman with *Neustadter Brothers* in 1873, he became a principal partner following his patenting of a double thickness of material inside the pocket tops.

Other inventors and pants manufacturers followed. By 1880, at least ten other types of strengthened work pants were being made in San Francisco and sold across the West. Some of the inventors were, like Jacob Greenebaum, principal partners in established clothing firms. Some, like David Neustadter, were given a principal partnership in recognition of their inventions. Others started businesses manufacturing their newly designed and patented pants, like Berthold Greenebaum, who started the *Steam Men's Furnishing Goods Factory* with his brother(?) Oscar.

However, many who became involved in the competition to design improved work pants did not seek ownership shares; the largest group of inventors sold their patented designs to existing companies. Some were employed by the companies who bought their designs—like Antonio Diaz Peña, who worked as a clerk for *W. & I. Steinhart & Co.*, and Leon Aronson who was a salesman for *Toklas, Brown & Co.* Others were inventors who, somehow, found a company willing to pay them for their idea and put it into production. Rodmond Gibbons was one of those; he had several patents granted in the 1860s for ideas unrelated to clothing. Then, in 1876, he came up with the idea of extending the outside seam of the pocket vertically to strengthen the corner and sold it to *A. B. Elfelt & Co.* A partial pair of these pants that has a label with the manufacturer's name and patent number on it is known to exist.

For a number of reasons, it is rare to find examples of some of the types described above with an intact label. Fortunately, surviving records often clearly identify the manufacturing company for a given design, and one may deduce the origin of a particular example through cross-referencing. For instance, Samuel Krause's second patent for extending the ends of the rear cinch strap all the way around to reinforce the front pocket tops was assigned to *A. B. Elfelt & Co.*, making identification of these pants relatively easy. In contrast, identifying the manufacturer of Krause's earlier similar patent design of 1875 is done by inference: he was working as a foreman for *Greenebaum Brothers* at the time, but he soon went into his own business.

To an extent, the classification of remnants of old jeans is speculative, because there are no records to establish for certain when and by whom they were made. In writing this book, I have sometimes had to draw inferences based on my own research and observation, with consideration of information provided by available sources. If the record is strongly suggestive of a link between inventor and manufacturer, then an assumption is made. For instance, the link between Antonio Diaz Peña and *W. & I. Steinhart & Co.* is assumed based on the record that shows Antonio as a stock clerk with the company, living at 138 Silver Street in 1877—the year after his patent. But, the next year, he was a superintendent with the company, living at the Palace Hotel. It seems reasonable to assume that his dramatic rise in the company was related to his patent.

Similarly, the link between Chean Quan Wo and *Heynemann & Co.* is assumed based on the illustration accompanying Hermann Heynemann's 1881 patent. Although Hermann's patent was for reinforced work-pants knees, a drawing of a full pair of pants was used in the illustration. That illustration clearly shows Wo's 1874 patent design of triangular extensions of material reinforcing the pocket corners. Chean Quan Wo may have worked for *Heynemann & Co.* in the production lines, or more likely, as a foreman. A visitor describing San Francisco in 1877 commented, "In some [clothing] factories three hundred and even five hundred [Chinese men] are at work" (Kahn, 2002, p. 460). It is no surprise, then, that three of the patented designs for improved work pants in the 1870s were granted to Chinese men.

Collecting and learning about old jeans involves studying the history of San Francisco and the vast country in the inland mountains and deserts where gold and silver was found during the nineteenth century. Those of us who engage in this hobby (obsession?) find ourselves poring over old photos, newspapers, and files in search of snippets that, taken together, sometimes provide useful insights. The process of digging through records and comparing field notes with other collectors in an attempt to identify a swatch of old cloth is central to this field of interest. Sometimes, research reveals a surprising fact that contradicts prevailing notions. One always must bear in mind that what is known or believed about a particular person or manufacturer may be shown to be in error when the next discovery is made.

An ad for Dewey & Co. in Langley's 1868 San Francisco City Directory. (courtesy of San Francisco Public Library, History Center.)

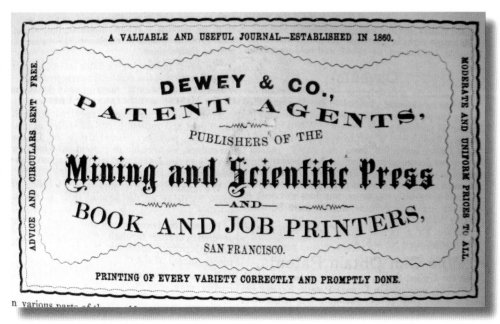

13

Inventors and manufacturers were not the only ones who played important roles in the competition for improved work pants. I must mention here the company that processed most of the patents granted to San Francisco inventors for improving the strength of work pants during the 1870s and 1880s—*Dewey & Co.* Twelve of the seventeen major patents were processed by *Dewey & Company*, including Jacob Davis' May 23, 1873, patent for riveting pants. The firm was first listed in San Francisco as a patent agency in 1864. The founder, Alfred T. Dewey, was born in Massachusetts in 1834 and came to California sometime before 1860. He was a printer by trade and first set up in California in the mining town of La Porte before moving to San Francisco. While in business in San Francisco, he entered into two other enterprises besides his patent agency: magazine publishing (*The Mining and Scientific Press*, *Pacific Rural Press*, *Pacific States Watchman*, and *Ladies Home Journal*) and wood and photo engraving. Alfred died in the 1890s. [An interesting note: Joshua Abraham Norton, the famed self-proclaimed Emperor of the U.S. and Protector of Mexico, worked for *Dewey*

& Co. as a bookkeeper (Kahn, 2002 p. 447).] These were remarkable times indeed!

The known facts about some patent designs and their inventors are too sketchy to link them to a manufacturing company. Such is the case with Charles Jones, who patented a design of two layers of material in the top half of pants in 1879. Although, an example of the pants is known, the name of the manufacturer is not. Yung Chow invented a pocket rim lined with a reinforcing cord in 1878. Only a fragment of pants that are (possibly) of that design is known.

Then there are the inventors and companies about which very little is known. Harman Adams patented a strengthening idea for work pants in 1876; but not even fragments of this design are known, nor a company that may have made them. William G. Badger, proprietor of *William G. Badger & Co.*, trademarked the name "Hercules" for overalls in 1878. The name was obviously meant to be attached to strengthened work pants that would compete with Levi Strauss's riveted pants and the other San Francisco designs, but no patent can yet be associated with his company.

A changing room at a Nevada silver mine. Here, workers would put on work pants owned by the mine and leave them after their shift. This way "highgrading," carrying silver bullion off in their pockets, could be prevented. (courtesy of Special Collections Department, University of Nevada, Reno Library.)

The strengthened work pants made by *Levi Strauss & Co.* and other competing companies from 1873 to 1890 were sold in all the mining areas of the West. So far as is known, these pants were only made in San Francisco. They were probably marketed by company salesmen traveling to the dry-goods stores in the mining towns and boom camps. In addition to the retailers who bought pants, many of the silver mines and mills bought them in large numbers to be worn only during work shifts. This was to guard against "high grading" or theft of silver. The employees would have a changing room where they would put on the company clothes and leave their own. After their shift, the workers would change back into their clothes—probably under the watchful eye of an attendant.

Although *Levi Strauss & Co.'s* riveted work pants sold well in the mid-1870s, the other companies also had some success with their competing designs. To maintain its dominant position in the market, *Levi Strauss & Co.* continually improved its products. So, by the mid-1880s, the other companies were left to wait until the Levi Strauss patent ran out in 1890 when they too could make riveted pants. These other companies, then, only produced work pants strengthened by other designs, from about 1874 to the late 1880s. Although the record is lacking, it is safe to assume that many of these competing designs were made in limited production runs and not widely distributed. Accordingly, examples of these other types of pants are rare; some are only known from fragments.

I want to mention here the difficulties faced by work pants manufacturers in the East during the time of the boom in patent ideas in San Francisco from 1873 to 1890. The Eastern companies got left out of the loop, probably because of the great distance, and also because of the speed with which ideas were born, developed, patented, and put into production in San Francisco. By 1880, the patents for strengthening work-pants had covered most of the possibilities that were practical. Little was left for anyone else to patent. Some did try. J. Wahl of Chicago, Illinois, was an example. In 1883, he unsuccessfully tried to patent an idea for strengthening work pants pocket corners. The evidence for this is on the illustration for the patent he did get. The drawing of the pants shows not only his patentable invention for an adjustable waist design, but also a design for strengthening pocket corners. That idea was too similar to other inventions that had already been patented in San Francisco years earlier. Being unable to use his pocket strengthening idea for production he resorted to a simple, heavy stitch line across the pocket corners. A surviving pair of his pants (salesman's sample) is shown in the chapter Additional Nineteenth Century Clothing Items From the Old West. (Apparently, stitching variations, like the large triangular stitching on Neustadter Brothers "Boss of the Road" brand work pants, were not patentable.)

The following section contains chapters that focus on individual manufacturers. I begin with a chapter on the jeans made by *Levi Strauss & Co.*, with succeeding chapters devoted to other San Francisco clothing companies that manufactured work pants to compete with *Levi Strauss & Co.'s* riveted jeans. These chapters detail what is known about these scarce Western work pants of the 1870s and 1880s, the companies that made them, and the inventors who conceived of them. Where possible, photographs illustrating the details of various designs are included. In some cases, these examples are no more than fragments, but I value them highly for the information they provide. Many of these fragile artifacts have survived for over a hundred and thirty years after they were so worn out that they were discarded.

A photograph of visitors underground at a silver mine in the Comstock Lode near Virginia City, Nevada. (courtesy of Special Collections Department, University of Nevada, Reno Library.)

Levi Strauss & Company

Although the name "Levi Strauss" is known world-wide today, in 1870 *Levi Strauss & Co.* was only one of a hundred or more dry goods companies in San Francisco. In the latter half of the nineteenth century, Battery Street and Sansome Street were lined with three- and four-story buildings housing clothing company showrooms, warehouses, and offices. *Neustadter Brothers, Toklas, Hahn and Brown*, and *Heynemann & Co.* were there. *W. & I. Steinhart* were neighbors at 3 and 5 Battery Street. *Levi Strauss & Co.* moved to 14 and 16 Battery Street in 1866—shown in the accompanying photograph (Courtesy of the San Francisco Public Library, History Center). These businesses mainly sold goods shipped from the East Coast; San Francisco had yet to develop as a manufacturing center for work-men's clothing.

Levi Strauss sailed to San Francisco in 1853 to expand the family business into the markets created by the gold rush. His two older brothers, Jonas and Louis, stayed in New York and managed their dry

16

goods firm—Strauss Brothers (Marsh, Trynka, & Marsh, 2005, p. 12 & 13). During Levi's first year in San Francisco, he started *Levi Strauss & Company* on California Street, between Sansome and Battery. Many of the goods he sold were shipped to him by the Strauss business in New York. This was the same for most of the dry goods companies in San Francisco at the time; labor was too expensive in California to locally manufacture goods that could be shipped from the East Coast, where labor was cheap (Cray, 1978, p. 11). While the manufacture of ready-made work pants was one enterprise that specifically benefited from cheap labor, other 'gents' furnishing goods' that would have to be personally fitted, like dress shirts, could be made in San Francisco by tailors. Eventually, factories were established for these items—*Neustadter Brothers* set up the *Standard Shirt Factory* in 1875.

So, in the 1850s and 1860s, if you purchased a pair of jeans from a San Francisco dealer, they were likely made in New York. The pants would have had a small cinch strap in the back for adjusting the waist fit (belt loops wouldn't be added for several decades). This cinch strap was buckled across a "V" notch in the waist of the pants. The pants would also have had a set of suspender buttons along the waistband (which were almost never used by miners; they would use a piece of rope tied around their waist instead of using suspenders). But, the pants would not have had a watch pocket or a back pocket. These ready-made work pants wore out rapidly and would have had to be replaced often (or repaired until they were ready to fall off). Levi Strauss and his competitors sold these pants to miners in the gold camps of California and mining camps all over the West. They were meant to be worn by men engaged in heavy labor They were not intended to be worn on the city streets or as every-day wear. These pants were strictly for work, and, as mentioned above, some silver reduction mills bought these work pants to be worn by their employees only during work shifts. After use, the pants would be left hanging in changing rooms where they would don their own pants to wear home.

For twenty years, Levi Strauss sold imported work pants in competition with the other San Francisco wholesale clothing companies around him. Then, in 1872, Jacob Davis approached Levi Strauss with a new idea for making waist overall work pants—using copper rivets. At the time, Jacob was working out of his tailor shop in Reno, Nevada. In a letter to Levi, Jacob described his idea and asked Levi for help in patenting his invention for a share of the rights (Cray, 1978, p. 20 & 21). With the benefit of hindsight, it is obvious that Davis' idea for riveted pants, and the partnership formed between Davis and Levi Strauss to produce the pants, would take on enormous importance in the full-

ness of time. Not surprisingly, controversy surrounds the historical record of these events.

There have been several stories about the discovery of riveted pants. An early one had Levi Strauss himself making the discovery; however, most versions in the twentieth century focused on Jacob Davis. The most common story was of a prospector named Alkali Ike who complained to Jacob that the seams of his pants pockets were always ripping out when he carried rocks in them. Jacob went to a blacksmith, as the story goes, and had him rivet the pocket corners with square iron nails. Versions of this story were printed in magazines and *Levi Strauss & Co.* brochures in the 1950s. These stories probably came from popular myth.

Perhaps, the most reliable source was tapped by Ed Cray for his 1978 book *Levi's* (p. 18, 265, & 266). In 1874, Jacob Davis gave testimony in a suit against A. B. Elfelt & Co. for patent infringement. According to Cray, in the transcript, Jacob tells of getting the idea while making a pair of pants for a neighbor. The neighbor's wife had requested a strong pair of pants for her husband, so Jacob used the strongest material he had in the shop—10oz duck that he had been using for making horse blankets. (*See the definition of "duck" in the chapter on Denim Manufacturing.*) Sitting in the place he usually sat to make the blankets, he finished sewing the pants, and lying before him on the table were the copper rivets he used on the horse blankets. Davis' statement concluded, "...And the thought struck me to fasten the pockets with those rivets."

Following his initial experiment with the neighbor's pants, Jacob made more riveted waist work pants for sale out of his Reno shop beginning in early 1871. The sales of his rugged pants increased rapidly; he reportedly sold at least 200 pair by the time he approached Levi Strauss (Cray, 1978, p. 19). As the popularity of his design grew, Davis became concerned about protecting his intellectual property.

But, in 1872, Jacob Davis recognized that he needed help patenting his idea for riveting work pants; and, I suspect that Jacob sought Levi Strauss' help not just for the cost of the patent, but perhaps mostly for protecting it in court against infringement--a cost that Jacob probably could not have afforded. Indeed, two suits for infringement did follow after it was patented; one against *A. B. Elfelt & Co.*, a large San Francisco clothing manufacturer, and the other against Kan Lun, a small business man in San Jose (Cray, 1978, p. 24).

Levi Strauss agreed to help Jacob with his patent and asked him to come to San Francisco to supervise the production of the pants for the company. In May of 1873, a patent for using copper rivets to strengthen waist overall work pants was granted to Jacob W. Davis and assigned to himself and *Levi Strauss & Company*. (The

Levi Strauss & Co. ad from the May 9, 1874. *Tehama Independent* newspaper. (Tehama County, California).

oversight of not including other clothing, such as blouses, was corrected in 1875 by a reissue of the patent).

To convey a sense of the kind of man Jacob Davis was, it is worth noting that Jacob Davis was the second-most prolific inventor, of the group that came up with improvements for jeans, after Rodmond Gibbons (see *A. B. Elfelt & Company* chapter). In addition to his patented design for riveted pants, Davis invented a corn sheller in 1866 and an ironing-stretcher in 1871. He also patented a further improvement for jeans in 1878, while he was working for *Levi Strauss & Co.*

Beginning in 1873, both 10oz. duck and 9oz. denim pants were manufactured under the supervision of Jacob Davis as foreman of *Levi Strauss & Co.'s* new production line. The revolutionary pants had a leather label in the center of the back on the waistband with the words: "LEVI STRAUSS & CO. SOLE PROPRIETORS AND MANUFACTURERS OF THE PATENTED RIVETED DUCK AND DENIM PANTS." The company copyrighted the label on February 10, 1874. The label was probably modified to read "…DUCK AND DENIM CLOTHING" sometime in 1874 to include blouses and

other riveted items. And, perhaps about that time, more information was added to the label. I surmise this because the labels got larger (but, unreadable). The *Levi Strauss & Co.* billhead from May 7, 1880, shown has a label in the upper right that may have the same wording as that early jeans label, but with the Company name and address added.

By the late 1880s, the label read: "LEVI STRAUSS & CO. – 14 AND 16 BATTERY ST, SAN FRANCISCO, CAL – SOLE PROPRIETORS AND MANUFACTURERS OF PATENTED RIVETED DUCK AND DENIM CLOTHING, SECURED LETTERS PATENTED MAY 20, 1873, RENEWED MARCH 16, 1875 – EVERY PAIR GUARANTEED – NONE GENUINE UNLESS BEARING THIS TRADEMARK – ANY INFRINGEMENTS OF THIS PATENT WILL BE PROSECUTED TO THE FULLEST EXTENT OF THE LAW – LABEL COPYRIGHTED."

The appearance of Levi Strauss & Co.'s copper-riveted jeans in the market must have sent a shock through the offices of their competitors. Since about 1858, dry goods stores in Nevada had been purchasing large numbers of waist overall work pants to sell to the silver mines and mills. This was very likely a source of large profits for the San Francisco dealers, as the pants could be made cheaply and had to be replaced often.

What did those first riveted jeans look like? I can give a fairly accurate description of them using very early fragments that I have seen. Unlike earlier non-riveted waist overall work pants, they had a back pocket and a watch pocket above the right front pocket, and the waistband did not have a "V" notch in the back. These few, simple features would have added value to the pants and made them easily distinguishable from other brands. I have put together a group of photographs of what I think are very early examples of riveted denim (1873 or 1874) and duck (1875 or 1876) waist overall work pants made by *Levi Strauss & Co.*

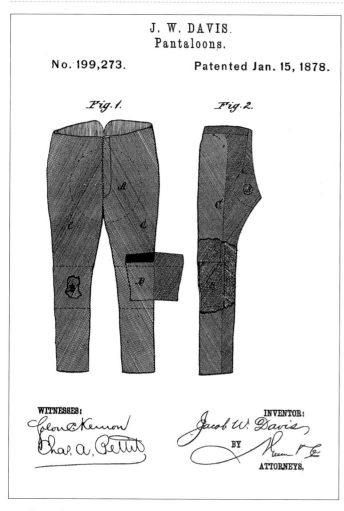

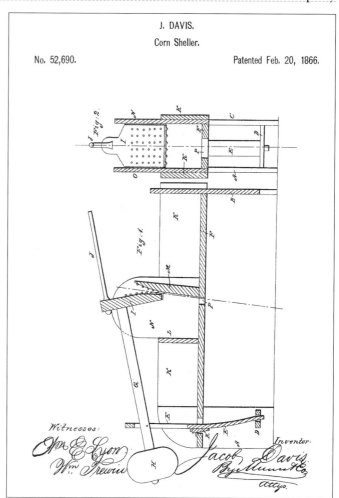

Jacob Davis also improved on the knees of work pants with this invention in 1878.

Jacob Davis had several patents before his rivet patent of 1873. This one was for a corn kernel removal invention.

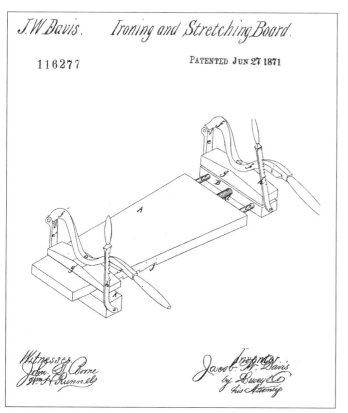

Another earlier patent by Jacob Davis—a stretcher board for pants.

J. W. DAVIS.
Fastening Pocket-Openings.

No. 139,121.

Patented May 20, 1873.

Fig. 1.

The patent that started it all. The
denim jeans were born in much their
modern form by this patent design using the rivet for strengthening. (*This and
all subsequent patents shown in the book are
from the United States Patent Office.*)

Witnesses

Inventor

A pair of Levi Strauss & Co. waist overall work pants made of duck. According to an 1879 price list, their duck pants came in three colors—brown, mode, and deadgrass. [Mode was a drab gray]. There is a small watch pocket above the left front pocket, and all of the pockets are riveted at the top corners. The front pocket tops are curved downward. The pants are tentatively dated to 1875 or 1876.

The back of the pair of riveted duck work pants. It has one back pocket, riveted at the top corners, but the cinch strap is not riveted. The dating of this pair to 1875 or 1876 is based partly on the design of the cinch strap attachments. There is no arcuate stitch on the back pocket.

Close-up of the top front of the 1875-76 duck pants to show the front pocket bags (the left bag can be seen through a hole in the pants) were made of the same material as the pants.

A fragment of Levi Strauss & Co. riveted denim jeans with a Type III cinch strap attachment.

Close-up of the back pocket of the pair of jeans with the Type III cinch strap attachment. The faint arcuate stitch can be seen. This is the first appearance of the arcuate stitch that I have found.

Details of the watch pockets of the riveted 1874(?) denim pants and the riveted ca. 1875-76 duck pants, showing the position of the watch pocket tops—about half-way up on the waist band.

This very early Levi Strauss & Co. work pants fragment is made of heavy denim. There are two front pockets, a small watch pocket above the left front pocket, and all of the pockets are riveted at the top corners. The front pocket tops are curved downward. The pocket bags (the bottom of the left bag is partly showing) are made of the same material as the pants. These pants are tentatively dated to 1874.

The back of the same fragment in the previous photograph. It has one back pocket, riveted at the top corners. There is a gather of yoke material to the right of the cinch strap, and the cinch strap is not riveted. (The yoke is the long triangular pieces of material just below the back waistband, added to give a better fit).

Fragment of early (1874?) Levi Strauss & Co. denim work pants showing the leather label in the center of the back waistband. This one is not legible. The cinch strap is small and not riveted.

Close-up of the top back of the ca. 1875-76 Levi Strauss & Co. duck pants showing the Type III cinch strap and the position of the leather label (seen as the rectangular outline of thread that held the label on.)

Close-up of the cinch strap on a pair of Levi Strauss & Co. riveted jeans showing a Type II cinch strap attachment. The pocket is undecorated (no arcuate stitch).

Close-up of the back pocket of the Levi Strauss & Co. riveted 1874(?) denim (Type I cinch strap attachment). The pocket is undecorated (no arcuate stitch).

Close-up of the back pocket of the ca. 1875-76 duck pants (Type II cinch strap attachment). There is no arcuate stitch on the pocket.

The back pocket of the Levi Strauss & Co. riveted jeans with a Type II cinch strap attachment. The pocket is undecorated (no arcuate stitch).

Close-ups of the copper rivets showing the pre-1890 embossing on (nearly) all Levi Strauss & Co. rivets: PAT. MAY 1873 LS&CO. SF. Except for the very earliest examples, all of the pre-1890 Levi Strauss & Co. pants in this book have been identified by this embossing on the rivets.

As the illustrations demonstrate, these first *Levi Strauss & Co.* riveted jeans were very well made. The stitching was fine and straight. Jacob Davis, as factory foreman, must have kept a close eye on the quality of his products. The decision to employ several different methods of cinch strap attachment during the first few years of production was probably driven by a wish for superior goods. Surviving examples reveal that, for whatever reason, at first the cinch strap was not attached with rivets. Evidently, there was an effort by the company to strengthen that part of the pants by increasing the stitch area and the size of the cinch strap—until, finally, rivets were used. A more detailed explanation of these variations, and their possible use in dating early *Levi Strauss & Co.* jeans is given later in this chapter.

After the *Levi Strauss & Co.* pants came on the market, competing manufacturers realized that they would have to come up with their own strengthened work pants or lose customers to whom they had been selling for many years. At least one manufacturer tried marketing a "knock off" version of Davis' design. *A. B. Elfelt & Company* tried selling their version of riveted work pants, but was promptly sued by *Levi Strauss & Co.* in 1874. By taking strong, prompt action to stave off "copy cats," *Levi Strauss & Co.* sent a clear message that inventors would have to come up with other ideas.

In the next four years, there were nine separate patents granted for designs to strengthen the pockets of waist overall work pants in ways other then riveting. Another six were granted by the end of 1881. The other companies on Battery and Sansome streets found ways to make work pants that could be sold by their salesmen to dry goods stores in the hundreds of towns and mining camps of the West. Although none of these companies would overtake *Levi Strauss & Co.*, the few known remnants of their products bear witness to the creativity and skill they brought to the contest. Unfortunately, at present there are more questions than answers about these jeans and the people who made them. In the chapters that follow, I will share what I know about these lesser-known companies and the jeans that they marketed.

Aside from concerns about the cost of replacing pants that failed prematurely, *Levi Strauss & Co.'s* early efforts to improve their cinch-strap attachment may well have been driven by competition from other designers. The *Neustadter Brothers* design strengthened their cinch-strap attachments by curving them up under the waistband. The *Meyerstein & Lowenberg* design also tucked the ends under an enlarged waistband. *S. R. Krouse* went so far as to extend the ends of the cinch strap around to the front of the pants; and, his second design extended them all the way to the tops of the front pockets. *A. B. Elfelt & Co.* enlarged the at-

tachment ends of their cinch strap so much that they looked like butterfly wings.

If the first riveted jeans made by *Levi Strauss & Co.* had a flaw that made them inferior to those of their rivals, it was the cinch strap attachment. This was no minor concern: in the strongly competitive atmosphere of the times, any selling point could be an advantage. A *Levi Strauss & Co.* in-house letter noted in 1881 that "...all the clothing houses have worked very hard against us..." The riveting and enlarging of the cinch strap was the main change during the early years of Levi Strauss & Co. jeans production, which also saw the addition of the arcuate stitch on the back pocket. (The arcuate stitch is the trademark rounded "m" shaped or gull-wing stitching on the back pocket.) By the late 1870s, the production lines of *Levi Strauss & Co.*, under the supervision of Jacob Davis, were turning out work pants that were superior in every way to any that had ever been made—or were being made by other companies of the time.

One must exercise a degree of caution when making firm statements about a specific feature of a given manufacturer's pants, as unexpected variations turn up periodically. The next group of photographs shows a pair of waist overall work pants made by *Levi Strauss & Co.* around 1877. This particular pair

has a tool pocket on the side of the left leg. Several fragments of this type have been found, and they all could be from about the same time period—from about 1876 to 1878. It may be that the tool pocket was a regular feature on the *Levi Strauss & Co.* work pants during that time.

Close-up of the crotch area showing the peculiar "7" stitch to the right of the rivet that goes behind the top edge of the rivet. This stitch pattern is on all early Levi Strauss & Co. work pants that I have seen.

Close inspection of the tool pocket waist overall work pants shown in the series of photographs reveal them to be superior to anything the other San Francisco companies were selling. The quality of the material, stitching, and construction is remarkable. Other than the improvement in the cinch-strap attachment, there were almost no changes from the jeans *Levi Strauss & Co.* had made in 1873.

By 1877, several of the other manufacturers of "gents' furnishing goods" in San Francisco had developed their own improved waist overall work pants, but the superiority of the riveted jeans of *Levi Strauss & Co.* must have made it difficult to market their non-riveted pants. The scarcity of non-riveted, strengthened work pants dating from the late 1870s to the late 1880s, is evidence of the market dominance *Levi Strauss & Co.* enjoyed during this period.

After 1890, waist overall denim work pants made by *Levi Strauss & Co.* were little changed from the late 1870s. I show one example for comparison.

Back of the same pair of pants. The only obvious changes from the earlier Levi Strauss & Co. pants are the rivets in the cinch strap and the small "tool pocket" on the leg.

A pair of late 1870s (1876-77?) denim waist overall "tool-pocket" work pants made by Levi Strauss & Co. This front view, when compared to the early 1870s pairs, shows very little change. All of the rivets are embossed on both sides with the patent date.

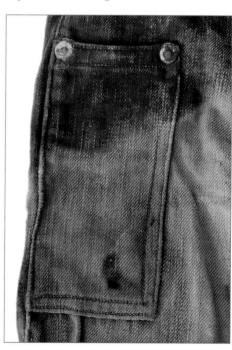

Close-up of the fifth "tool pocket." Because it's on the side of the right leg, I surmise that it may have been added for miners to carry a chisel.

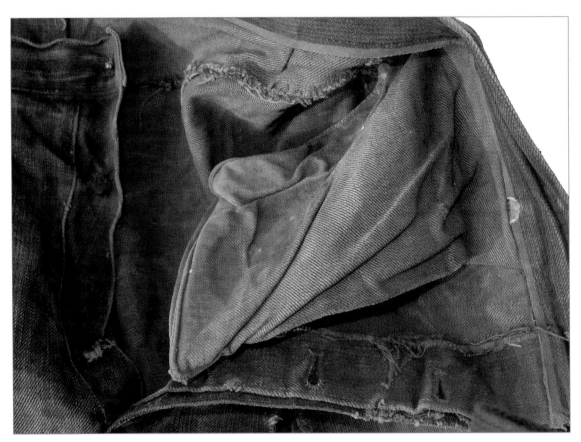

The inside of the "tool pocket" pants, showing the denim pocket bags—same as earlier Levi Strauss & Co. work pants.

Close-up of the watch pocket on the "tool pocket" pants. The top of the watch pocket may be a little lower than on earlier pants.

Close-up of the top back of the "tool pocket" pants showing the label location and the riveted cinch strap.

Close-up of the crotch area of the "tool pocket" pants showing the peculiar "7" stitch pattern to the right of the rivet.

Close-up of the back pocket on the "tool pocket" pants. A faint arcuate stitch can be seen on the pocket.

This pair of Levi Strauss & Co. jeans is dated as post-1890 by the embossing on the rivets—"LS & CO SF." This embossing presumably began in 1890 when the patent for riveting pants expired—seventeen years after the patent was granted. It has one label in the center of the back waistband, the pocket bags are denim, and it has the arcuate stitch on the back pocket. The only major difference between this pair and the ca. 1877 "tool pocket" pair is that the cinch strap is riveted on one side only. Levi Strauss & Co. made several lines of jeans by this time. This is a pair of their heavy denim work pants.

Back of post-1890 Levi Strauss & Co. heavy denim work pants. The label is still in the center of the back of the waistband, but the cinch strap is riveted only on the right side.

Inside top of post-1890 Levi Strauss & Co. heavy denim work pants. The pocket bags are still made of denim.

Some mention should be made of the other riveted clothing that *Levi Strauss & Co.* made in the 1870s. Apparently, the intention at first was to manufacture riveted work pants only, as the original patent only specified pants. But, in 1875, the patent was reissued to include other articles of clothing. In fact, in 1874, Jacob Davis and Levi Strauss had applied for a patent for riveted "wearing apparel" in the United Kingdom and had included illustrations of a vest and a hunting coat. I assume that their line of riveted clothing also included blouses (an old term for jackets) by this time. The following are photographs of a blouse made by *Levi Strauss & Co.*, about 1874 or 1875. This estimated date of manufacture is based on the method of attaching (sewing or riveting on) the cinch strap (shown in the second photograph).

Close-up of the back of the Levi Strauss & Co. blouse showing the cinch strap attachment. This is a Type II attachment, dating this blouse to about 1874 or 1875. The label is missing on the lower edge of the blouse, but probably was the same as the waist overall work pants of the same period.

The preceding sections provide a context for understanding the dynamics that drove the growth of the work clothing business in San Francisco, and how *Levi Strauss & Co.* came to dominate the market. Before going on to the chapters about the makers and inventors of the non-riveted jeans, I would like to focus on some of the details about the jeans made by *Levi Strauss & Co.*: to describe how I have tentatively dated the early examples of *Levi Strauss & Co.* work pants; to show some other early variations in their construc-tion; and, lastly, to present a unique pair of jeans that I believe to be very early *Levi Strauss & Co.* jeans. Some of this information will be of interest mainly to collectors; however, I believe that by taking a closer look at the details that characterize various stages in the development of the pants themselves, even the casual reader will appreciate the efforts made by Levi Strauss and Jacob Davis to continually improve their products. These people were determined to remain first in their field.

Dating of Early Levi Strauss & Company Jeans

Variations in the cinch straps on early examples of *Levi Strauss & Co.* jeans demonstrate that this feature underwent rapid evolution, and it often is possible to identify and date a specimen by examining the cinch strap. Among the examples of early *Levi Strauss & Co.* work pants, there is a group that has differences in the design of the cinch strap compared with all later work pants. Three of these design types have rivetless cinch straps and one has rivets. I assume that the pants with an unriveted cinch strap were made first, and rivets were added later. These differences may give some indication of the relative age of pants during the first few years of production. The variations in the construction of the cinch strap seem to allow for a logical order. They can be arranged so that each change is a small step stronger than the preceding in the strength of the attachment points. I have provided a diagram showing the stitch patterns, sizes, and rivets on the variations I have seen that I will call Types I through IV (earliest to latest). Type V is the common construction found in all later *Levi Strauss & Co.* pants.

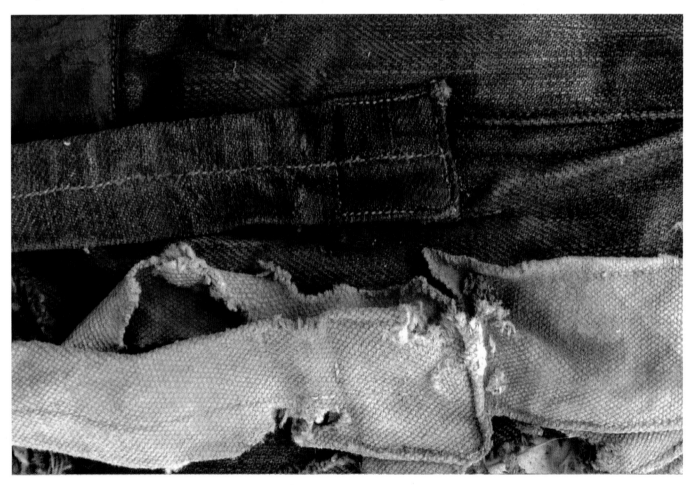

This photograph shows the size difference between the Type I denim and Type I duck cinch strap attachments.

Comparison of a Type III cinch strap attachment (above) with a Type I.

Comparison of a Type II cinch strap attachment (above) with a Type III.

A stacking of the top backs of seven pairs of Levi Strauss & Co. waist overall work pants in assumed date order from earliest at the top to the youngest at the bottom. The cinch straps are aligned to show the differences. The top two are denim Type I cinch straps, the third from the top is a duck Type I cinch strap. Type II is not shown. The fourth and fifth from the top are denim and duck Type III cinch straps. The second from the bottom is a denim Type IV cinch strap, and at the bottom is a Type V cinch strap in duck.

Comparison of a Type I cinch strap attachment (above) with a Type V.

This ordering, then, allows for a relative dating of the examples. If it is assumed that this series of changes in cinch-strap construction took place over about three or four years, from 1873 to 1877, allowing about one year for each variation, then some specific dates can be estimated. The addition of the arcuate stitch could be dated to 1875 or 1876 because of its first appearance on a Type III denim pair (none of the Type I or Type II pants I have seen have an arcuate stitch on the back pocket). However, several examples of duck work pants with a Type III cinch strap do not have an arcuate stitch on the back pocket. *Levi Strauss & Co.* may have delayed putting the arcuate stitch on the heavier duck work pants. The appearance of the tool pocket line (fifth pocket) may tentatively be dated to about 1876 or 1877, because one of the examples has a Variant IV cinch strap.

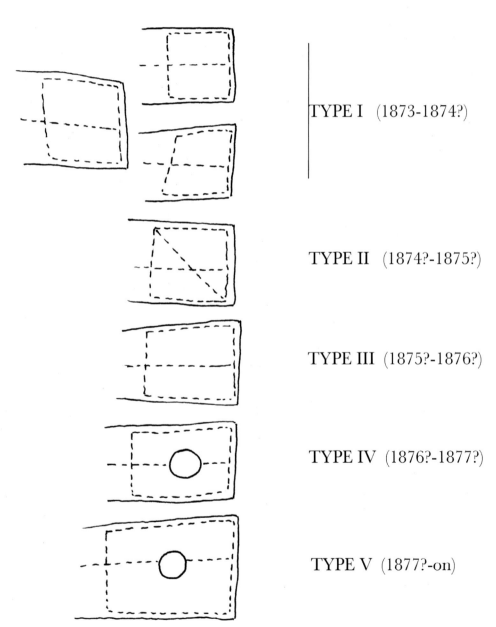

TYPE I (1873-1874?)

TYPE II (1874?-1875?)

TYPE III (1875?-1876?)

TYPE IV (1876?-1877?)

TYPE V (1877?-on)

This diagram shows all five types of cinch strap attachment designs in the first few years of production of Levi Strauss & Co. work pants. Each one was traced from a pair of pants so the sizes are proportional. Starting at the top, the earliest, or Type I, is a simple box-like stitch pattern. Jeans with unmarked rivets all have Type I cinch strap attachments. This first box stitch was sometimes skewed into more of a parallelogram as shown by the one below it. The Type I pattern was sometimes a little larger on the duck pants as shown by the tracing to the left of the two Type Is. Type II, shown next below, is a larger box pattern on a larger cinch strap with a diagonal stitch added. Type III, next below, is elongated into a rectangle, but without a diagonal stitch. The arcuate pocket stitch first appears on Type III. Type IV is the first riveted attachment, which is over a Type III stitch pattern. And, last, Type V is the cinch strap attachment seen on all later Levi Strauss & Co. work pants in the 1870s. I have tentatively assigned dates to the different types, allowing about one year for each.

Other Early Variations

There were other variations in the construction of *Levi Strauss & Co.'s* waist overall work pants in the first few years. Minor variations such as leather-backed rivets were seldom seen, while some variations survived as separate lines such as the horse blanket-lined duck waist overalls.

The watch pocked evolved in much the same way as the cinch strap, and may be used (albeit with less precision) to approximate the manufacture date of a particular specimen. The position of the small watch pocket shows an irregular, but inevitable lowering over time. In the 1870s, it was positioned with the top about half way up on the waistband; but on some examples it is slightly lower. Sometime after 1890, the top of the watch pocket was positioned below the waistband. The only possible reasons for the changes in the small watch pocket position that I can propose are, at first, a wish to keep the small watch pocket out of the way of access to the large right front pocket (high on the waistband) and, perhaps the desire to facilitate access to the small pocket by lowering it. A small watch pocket near the top edge of the pants can be devilishly difficult to open. It seems, though, that the exact position of the top of the small watch pocket was not a strictly controlled design feature in the early years of production.

There also were a few rare variations in the rivets. I have seen some with the embossing "PAT May 1873 LS&CO SF" on the inside part of the rivet, but not on the outside part. One of these pants with one-side embossed rivets is the blanket-lined duck pair shown here. It is tentatively dated as 1873-74.

At least two pair of *Levi Strauss & Co.* denim waist overall work pants have been found that have rivets with the outside part made of brass like the one shown above. The rivets came in two parts: the part with a raised post in the center that was inserted through a hole from the inside of the pants and the "donut" that was placed over the post which was hammered out to affix it. The rivets were normally made of copper. One copper rivet embossed with the patent date tested 97.18% copper and 2.73% zinc. The zinc was probably added by the foundry to make the copper more rigid, making it alloyed copper. To be considered brass, about twice as much zinc would have had to be added.

Some denim-overall rivets have been found with leather between the rivet and the denim material, but it is rarely encountered.

A line that was probably started very early was the duck overalls with a horse blanket inner lining. I have seen only one example from the 1870s. The three photographs illustrate this example. It is just a fragment, but it does preserve important parts—a piece of the cinch strap and a piece of the back pocket.

A Levi Strauss & Co. brass rivet with the patent date embossed on it. This is the outside part of the rivet. The inside part is copper, as can be seen by the redder color of the center post.

A leather-backed rivet on a fragment of denim waist overalls. The cinch strap design on this pair of pants is Type IV—tentatively dating it to 1876-77. I have seen a leather-backed rivet on only one other Levi Strauss & Co. denim work pants fragment.

The cinch strap on the horse blanket-lined duck pants fragment shown in the next photographs. It has a Type I attachment. A Type III denim cinch strap piece is below it for comparison.

A fragment of the back pocket from the same Levi Strauss & Co. horse blanket-lined duck waist overalls. This is one of the examples that have the rivets embossed on the inside only. There is no arcuate stitch on the back pocket of these pants.

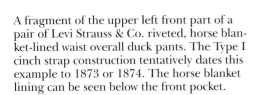

A fragment of the upper left front part of a pair of Levi Strauss & Co. riveted, horse blanket-lined waist overall duck pants. The Type I cinch strap construction tentatively dates this example to 1873 or 1874. The horse blanket lining can be seen below the front pocket.

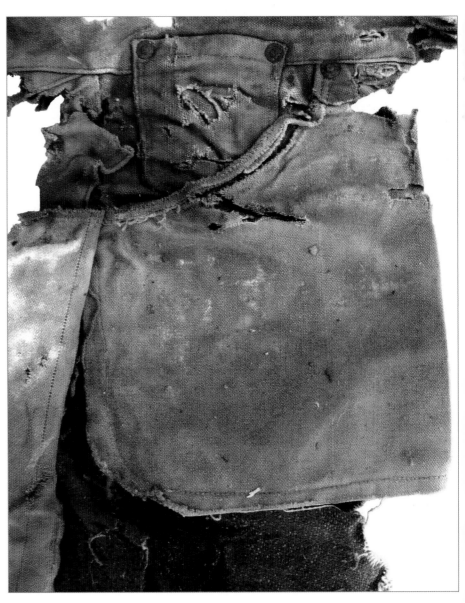

Unique Pair of Jeans

There is a pair of old waist overall denim work pants made with un-embossed rivets. I have reason to believe that they are very early *Levi Strauss & Co.*; perhaps the first few months of production. This would date the pants to 1873. The following photographs show these pants in some detail to illustrate their similarity to other early *Levi Strauss & Co.* jeans.

These riveted jeans were found in a trash pile in a Nevada mining town in 1969. They have a large original patch on the left leg. They are made of denim that is lighter than the usual denim used by Levi Strauss & Co. Today this type of denim is called 2 by 1 (see chapter on Wear Patterns of Nineteenth Century Work Wear for an explanation). The rivets are not embossed, which, along with other characteristics, makes me think that these are very early Levi Strauss & Co. jeans.

Back view of the very early riveted jeans. The holes in the legs and the missing part at the bottom of the right leg were caused by contact with pieces of iron in the trash pile, not original wear. Rust can be seen around most of the holes.

The top back of the very early jeans. The back pocket is a little smaller than the back pocket of most early Levi Strauss & Co. jeans. The "yoke" is the two elongate triangular pieces of material at the top of the pants, just below the back waistband. The yoke on this pair has a "gather" on each side; the same is found on all early Levi Strauss & Co. work pants such as the "tool pocket" pair shown in previous photographs. But, unlike, all but three examples I have seen of earliest Levi Strauss & Co. jeans, the yoke seam is on the outside at the pants seam (bottom edge of the yoke). There is no arcuate stitch on the rear pocket. In fact, these pants are devoid of any decorative stitching. Some of the other brands of work pants made in San Francisco in the 1870s, that I have seen, have decorative stitching on, at least, the front pockets. Only the very earliest Levi Strauss & Co. jeans were made plain, like these.

Close-up of the top of the back of the very early riveted jeans. The cinch strap attachment is like the Type I found on the earliest Levi Strauss & Co. jeans. The bright denim in the label area shows that the label was on this garment was found, but is now missing. It was probably made of leather and may have fallen off when they were picked up.

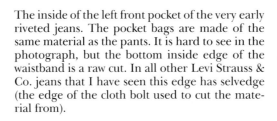

The inside of the left front pocket of the very early riveted jeans. The pocket bags are made of the same material as the pants. It is hard to see in the photograph, but the bottom inside edge of the waistband is a raw cut. In all other Levi Strauss & Co. jeans that I have seen this edge has selvedge (the edge of the cloth bolt used to cut the material from).

Close-up of left front pocket area of the very early riveted jeans. The top of the watch pocket is just above the mid-line of the waistband. This is a little higher than on any other pair of Levi Strauss & Co. jeans that I have seen. The missing rivet probably fell off due to the denim becoming weak around it during its residence in the trash pile.

The peculiar "7" stitch next to the crotch rivet is the same as on all 1870s Levi Strauss & Co. duck and denim waist overall work pants that I have seen.

Bottom of pant leg of very early riveted jeans folded out to show the selvedge on the denim edge.

Close-up of a rivet from the very early riveted jeans—unembossed.

Based on the characteristics I have described, I believe that this pair of pants was made by *Levi Strauss & Co.*, in the first months of production in San Francisco. The denim is lighter than the standard *Levi Strauss & Co.* used. The back pocket is a little smaller than what was standard on the *Levi Strauss & Co.* early riveted work pants. The watch pocket is slightly higher. And, the bottom edge of the waistband is raw-cut, whereas, on all other *Levi Strauss & Co.* denim jeans it is a selvedge edge. All of the other characteristics are the same, including some very small details such as the "7" stitch next to the crotch rivet. But, the rivets are unmarked.

Shown in detail is a peculiar stitch pattern on the cinch strap where the metal buckle is attached on the very early riveted pants. It is in the shape of a small rectangle or "box." The stitch pattern at this point on almost all other 1870s Levi Strauss & Co. work pants that I have seen is in the form of a "Z" as shown in the next photograph.

Detail of the metal buckle attachment on the cinch strap of an early pair of Levi Strauss & Co. jeans. This pair has the Type I (1873-74?) cinch strap construction. The "Z" was the common pattern for the stitching at this location. However, I have seen a couple of Levi Strauss & Co. work pants with a "box" stitch pattern here. The next photograph shows one.

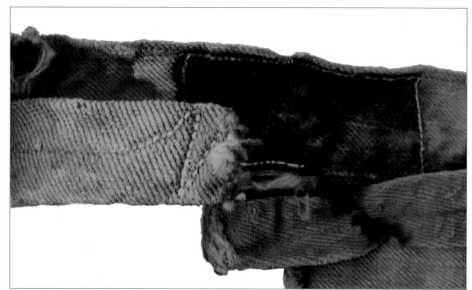

Detail of a metal buckle attachment "box" stitch on the cinch strap of a pair of Levi Strauss & Co. work pants tentatively dated to 1873-74 (Type I cinch strap). I have seen only one other example of this stitch pattern on a pair of denim "tool pocket" pants with a Type IV cinch strap (1876?-77?).

Summary of Early Jeans Made By Levi Strauss & Co.

First, I must mention that records from this time period—1873 to 1890—are scarce. The great San Francisco earthquake of 1906 and, especially, the fires started by it, wiped out much of the City, destroying any records from prior years. The photograph below shows the total devastation of the business district in and around the *Levi Strauss & Co.* building at 14 and 16 Battery Street.

This is why my story of the early development of jeans made by *Levi Strauss & Co.* is taken mainly from surviving examples—often fragments. Until new information surfaces, this is the story in brief:

Jacob Davis, the inventor of riveted jeans, came to San Francisco in 1873 to oversee the manufacturing of jeans for *Levi Strauss & Co.* He would have based this start-up production on the pants he had been making himself in Reno, Nevada, since 1871. The line of work pants would have included not only waist overalls in denim but also waist overalls in duck with and without a horse blanket lining.

During the first year of production, it would have become apparent that the unriveted cinch strap needed strengthening. After a few years of increasing its strength by increasing the size of the stitch pattern, the need for rivets was realized. After all, this was only available to *Levi Strauss & Co.* The other companies were going to great lengths to make strong cinch straps without using rivets. So, in about 1876 or 1877, both ends of the cinch strap were riveted.

During the first few years, someone in the company, perhaps a salesman, saw a benefit in adding an identifying mark on their jeans. Some of the other companies were adding decorative stitching on the pockets of their jeans. So, in about 1875 or 1876, Jacob Davis probably began specifying that the denim work pants be made with an arcuate stitch pattern on the back pocket (the gull-wing stitch pattern).

About the same time that the cinch strap was riveted, a small, extra pocket was added to the side of the leg. But, because it is not shown on the work pants in the illustration for an 1879 catalogue of *Levi Strauss & Co.* riveted products, I assume that it was discontinued by then.

By about 1879, the basic design of what would continue to be the standard *Levi Strauss & Co.* denim and duck waist overall work pants was set. And, this design was probably very much like the pants that Jacob Davis had first made in Reno, Nevada.

San Francisco Earthquake-Fire
April, 1906

Photograph of the Levi Strauss & Co. headquarters at 14 and 16 Battery Street taken soon after the San Francisco earthquake and fire in April 1906. The handwritten comment on the photograph—"all that remains of our store"—was probably penned by Levi Strauss's nephew, Jacob Stern, who took over management of the company on Levi's death in 1902. (courtesy of the Archives of Western States Jewish History—original source unknown.)

Small changes were made in the following 15 or 20 years. The cinch strap was sometimes reduced to one rivet on the right side (the pull side opposite the buckle). A line of heavier denim work pants was added. And, the trademark of two horses pulling on a pair of pants was added to the label (the label was still in the center of the waist band on the work pants line). On what was to become the 501™ line, the patch was moved to the side of the waist band and thin cotton pocket bags were used instead of denim. The ad with the new trademark shown is from around 1886.

Note the statement in the ad: "The only kind made by white labor." However, that was after 1877. Before that year, the workforce of the Levi Strauss & Co. production lines for riveted overalls was probably mostly Chinese. It was reported that Levi Strauss & Co. had 180 Chinese and 38 non-Chinese working in clothing manufacturing in November 1876. Sometime after the Chinatown riots in 1877, they employed only white labor in clothing production as the ad says. (courtesy of Glenn Mariconda)

Levi Strauss & Co. ad from the front page of the May 6, 1893, *Weekly Galt Gazette*, Sacramento County, California. (courtesy of Charla Harris)

Levi Strauss & Co. ad from the front page of the February 3, 1898, *Phoenix Weekly Herald*, Maricopa County, Arizona Territory. (courtesy of Charla Harris)

Greenebaum Brothers

The clothing manufacturer *Greenebaum Brothers* has a long and rich family history dating back to the early 1800s in Bavaria. There were six Greenebaum brothers, Levi, Abraham, Leon, Herman, Jacob, and Moses. They all immigrated to the U.S. between 1830-1847. *Greenebaum Brothers* was the third clothing business started by the brothers in the U.S. The first, *Greenebaum & Becker*, was a dry goods and clothing business started by Leon Greenebaum and a partner. This business was moved to San Francisco in 1851. The second was *Greenebaum & Brothers*, started by Jacob, Herman, and Moses in Sacramento. Those first two companies went through catastrophic fires that destroyed the stores. Leon was killed while trying to save his merchandise from the San Francisco fire. (Greenebaum family narrative, 1914)

The third business, which also took the name *Greenebaum Brothers*, was founded by Jacob, Herman, and Moses, and sold men's furnishing goods from 1868 to 1878. It was located on San Francisco's Market and Sutter streets. *Greenebaum Brothers* was in direct competition with *Levi Strauss & Company*. When Levi received the rivet patent on May 20, 1873, Jacob Greenebaum of *Greenebaum Brothers* was the first to apply for a patent that improved the strength and longevity of work pants without using rivets. His patent was for the application of triangular pieces of material (with one exception, only examples using leather have been found to date) to the same points where the Levi™ rivets were located. These "stress points" would wear quicker than other areas, so they were the natural focus of efforts by manufacturers to improve the strength of their pants. If companies could show that the durability, strength, and longevity of their jeans were improved, they would have a competitive edge over the others.

The early examples of these pants have smaller leather triangles than the later versions. The assumption was that the larger the pieces covering the stress points, the more durable the pants, thereby making Greenebaum's work pants more competitive with Levi's. The patent was also applied to blouses (the word used for jackets in the 1800s). The quality of the stitching observed on the Greenebaum work pants is not as high as that on Levi pants, meaning the stitching is not as tight and straight. *Greenebaum Brothers* work pants sold for quite a bit less than the Levi pants at the time. The *Morrison Brothers* ad from 1875, shown, gives a retail price of 75¢ per pair for "heavy leather bound overalls." This likely refers to Greenebaum Brothers pants, since they held the patent for this design.

The *Greenebaum Brothers* unique denim work pants appear to be the most common of the alternative pant designs that competed with the superior rivet design of *Levi Strauss & Company*. I base this assertion on the fact that I have encountered many more examples of these than any of the other competing brands. I assume that the successor companies–*Greenebaum, Sachs, and Freeman* (1878-1885) and

Moses Greenebaum

Jacob Greenebaum

Greenebaum, Weil, and Michels (after 1885) also manufactured the *Greenebaum Brothers* patented pant design—up until Jacob Davis's patent for riveted pants ran out in 1890. The building pictured was home to the *Greenebaum Brothers* and, afterwards, to *Greenebaum, Sachs, and Freeman*. The signs for both companies are on the building front. The brand name for these work pants was "Bodyguard." The cloth label for a pair made by *Greenebaum, Sachs & Freeman* is pictured in the "Additional Nineteenth Century Clothing Items from the Old West" chapter. No examples of the *Greenebaum Brothers* patented non-riveted jeans can be dated after 1890; so their production likely stopped when the riveted design became available to all.

Market Street directly opposite Second St. 1884

The ad in this 1875 newspaper for "HEAVY LEATHER BOUND OVER-ALLS" likely refers to Greenebaum Brothers pants that had leather triangles strengthening the pocket corners.

The fourth man from the right, in the top row, appears, under magnification, to be wearing a Greenebaum Brothers shirt with leather triangles on the top of the pocket corners. (*Note the young lad sporting a cigar in his mouth.*)

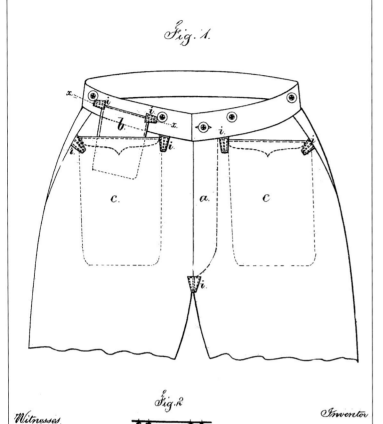

J. GREENEBAUM.

Overalls.

No.154,473.　　　　　　Patented Aug. 25, 1874.

Fig. 1.

Witnesses.　　　　　*Fig. 2.*　　　　*Inventor*

Chas H Smith　　　　　　　　　Jacob Greenebaum.

Harold Serrell　　　　　　　for Lemuel W. Serrell

　　　　　　　　　　　　　　　　　att'y.

Notice the mention of J. W. Davis in the 7th paragraph.

This is Jacob Greenebaum's patent granted in 1874 for strengthening pockets corners with "a re-enforcing lap" that was usually a leather triangle. This was the first patent to challenge Levi Strauss & Co.'s rivets. The leather triangles could be put on pants already in stock, and some pants with leather triangles applied appear to be of an older pre-1873 style.

Greenebaum Brothers

UNITED STATES PATENT OFFICE.

JACOB GREENEBAUM, OF SAN FRANCISCO, CALIFORNIA, ASSIGNOR TO GREENEBAUM BROTHERS.

IMPROVEMENT IN OVERALLS.

Specification forming part of Letters Patent No. **154,473,** dated August 25, 1874; application filed June 29, 1874.

To all whom it may concern:

Be it known that I, JACOB GREENEBAUM, of San Francisco, in the State of California, have invented an Improvement in Overalls, of which the following is a specification:

The pockets and flaps upon overalls are usually stitched upon the outside of the fabric composing the body of the overalls. Garments of this character are generally worn by workmen and subjected to very severe usage, and the angles of the pockets or ends of the flaps often give way and the lines of stitching break. The object of my invention is to strengthen the angles of the pockets and ends of the flaps, straps, or other pieces that are attached to the overall or similar garment—such as an over-jacket. For this purpose I employ a re-enforcing lap that covers the end of the lap or angle of the pocket, and extends from the same over and upon the surface of the body portion of the garment. Thereby the strain that comes upon the edge of the pocket or flap is not taken alone upon the stitching at the angle, but a portion thereof is taken by the re-enforce lap, and hence the angle or point of union of the two thicknesses of material is stronger and more durable.

In the drawing, Figure 1 is an elevation of the upper part of the front of the overalls, and Fig. 2 is a section at the line *x x*.

The overalls are made of any desired fabric and in the usual manner, except as hereafter named.

The flap *a* at the front is provided with but-

tons, the pocket *b* is stitched upon the outside of the fabric, and the pockets *c c* are inserted within the overalls, the upper end opening through the fabric. The re-enforcing laps *i i* are applied at the angles of the pockets and at the end of the flap, as represented.

This re-enforce lap is made, by preference, of a triangular form, and it is firmly sewed to place. It is applied so as to lap upon the flap or pocket, and also to extend upon the surface of the single fabric. Thereby the angle will be strengthened, and the strain transferred from the stitching of the flap or pocket to the re-enforce lap.

I am aware that the angles of pockets have been strengthened by metallic rivets, as in the patent of J. W. Davis, May 20, 1873, and such I do not claim; but

What I do claim as my invention is—

The overalls having the angles of the pockets and flap secured and strengthened by the re-enforce lap *i* of textile fabric, extending across such angles at the points of juncture, and secured to both portions of the fabric of which the overalls are composed, substantially in the manner described, and for the purposes set forth.

Signed by me this 24th day of June, A. D. 1874.

JACOB GREENEBAUM.

Witnesses:
GEO. T. PINCKNEY,
CHAS. H. SMITH.

49

A pair of Greenebaum Brothers pants with the patented triangular leather pieces (called re-enforce laps in the patent) sewn at the pocket corners.

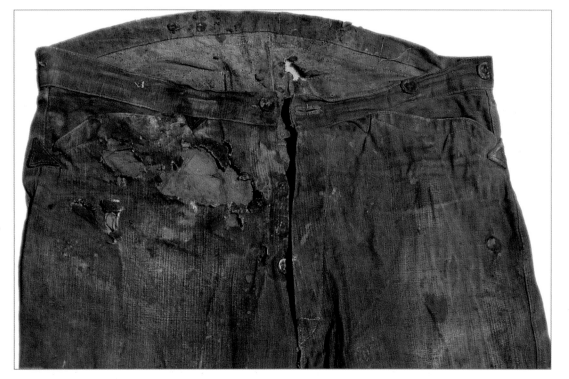

Top front of the Greenebaum Brothers pants. It does not have a watch pocket, suggesting that these pants were not made in San Francisco.

Top back of the Greenebaum Brothers pants. The cinch strap is relatively small, indicating an early date. The lack of a split in the back, though, suggests that these were not the earliest of this design, as examples are known that have a split back.

Right front pocket of the Greenebaum Brothers jeans. The cut of the pocket top suggests that they may not have been manufactured in San Francisco. Note the design stitch, which is typical of early Greenebaum Brothers jeans.

Back pocket of the Greenebaum Brothers pants. Note the uneven stitching around the pocket edge.

A pair of pre-1873-type light denim work pants that may have been sold by Greenebaum Brothers. The design stitch on the front pockets is typical of early Greenebaum Brothers pants, like the ones on the previously pictured example. I am speculating that these are pre-1873 pants manufactured on the East Coast and shipped to Greenebaum Brothers in San Francisco.

Top front of the pre-1873 Greenebaum Brothers(?) work pants. The pocket interiors are formed of a single layer of cotton cloth sewn to the inside of the pant legs. Most jeans made after 1873 had separate pocket bags.

Top back of the pre-1873 Greenebaum Brothers(?) pants. The split back, small cinch strap, and lack of a back pocket suggest that these were made before 1873.

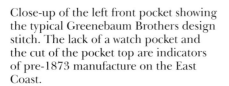

Close-up of the left front pocket showing the typical Greenebaum Brothers design stitch. The lack of a watch pocket and the cut of the pocket top are indicators of pre-1873 manufacture on the East Coast.

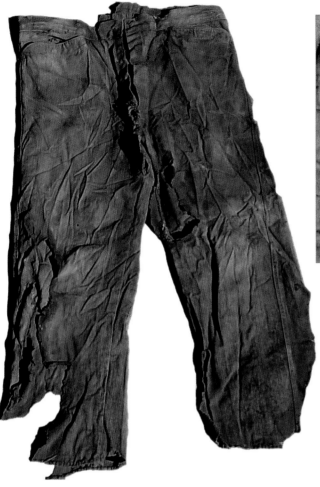

These pants had a back pocket that has been torn off. The shadows of the leather triangles at the pocket corners can be seen.

This pair of Greenebaum Brothers denim work pants is similar to the first pictured pair with patented leather triangles (re-enforce laps) at the pocket corners.

Top front of the same pair of pants. The lack of a watch pocket and the cut of the pocket tops lead me to think that these were made soon after the patent year of 1874, and not in San Francisco.

Close-up of the right front pocket showing the decorative stitch that is typical of early Greenebaum Brothers jeans.

This right front pocket of a pair of Greenebaum Brothers denim work pants can be compared with the one shown in the next picture. The cut of the pocket top shown here is typical of the pre-1873 work pants that I presume were imported from the East. Greenebaum Brothers may have used those pants by affixing the patented leather triangles on the pocket corners to sell out of their San Francisco store.

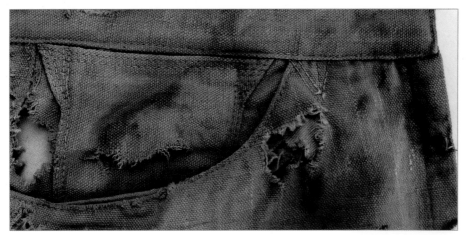

The right front pocket on, what I presume to be, a later pair of Greenebaum Brothers duck work pants. The cut of this pocket top is typical of work pants made in San Francisco after 1873. This pair of pants has another characteristic of post-1873 San Francisco-made work pants—a watch pocket—shown in the next picture. These later Greenebaum Brothers work pants also lack a decorative stitch on the pocket.

This close-up of the watch pocket on the later pair of Greenebaum Brothers duck work pants shows the design that I refer to as a "dog-eared" watch pocket. It does not appear to use leather triangles to fasten the top pocket corners down, but, rather, multiple stitch lines in a triangular form on pocket corner projections.

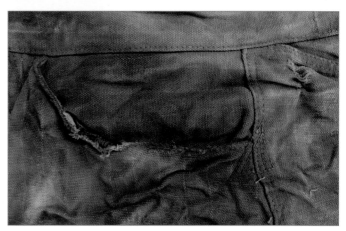

Breast pocket on a Greenebaum Brothers denim blouse. This is the only example I have seen that has the patented triangles at the pocket corners made of cloth instead of leather. This may have been a later development.

Close-up of one of the cloth triangle "re-enforce laps." The shape of the cloth triangle and its placement on the pocket corner is a little different than the leather triangles I have seen.

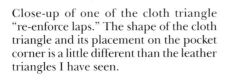

The back of a Greenebaum Brothers pullover (shirts that button halfway down the front). I have not yet seen a cinch strap on a Greenebaum Brothers pullover. Most other companies put cinch straps on their pullovers at this time.

The inside pocket of the Greenebaum Brothers pullover—made of a pillowcase-type material.

55

A Greenebaum Brothers denim jacket or blouse that has patented leather triangles on the corners of both breast pockets.

Left breast pocket showing a remaining leather "re-enforce lap."

Two Greenebaum Brothers denim pullovers with patented leather triangles on the pocket corners. Often they had only one breast pocket and a "Chinese style" collar.

This Greenebaum Brothers duck jacket has a significant amount of tar on it, suggesting that it came from a mine.

This pocket is from another Greenebaum Brothers duck jacket to illustrate the leather triangles. Duck jackets made by Greenebaum Brothers may have come in three colors— brown, mode, and deadgrass, like Levi Strauss & Co. duck jackets.

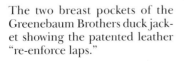

The two breast pockets of the Greenebaum Brothers duck jacket showing the patented leather "re-enforce laps."

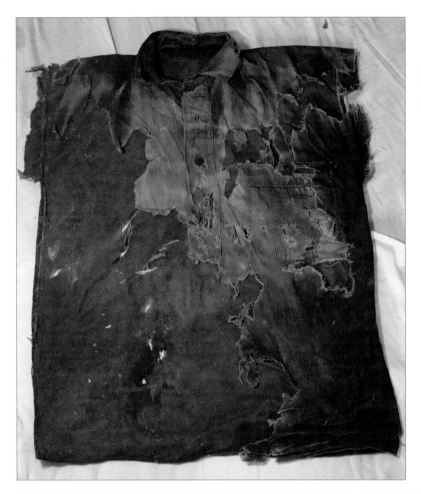

A pullover made by Greenebaum Brothers with their patented leather "re-enforce laps" at the pocket corners.

Back of the collar.

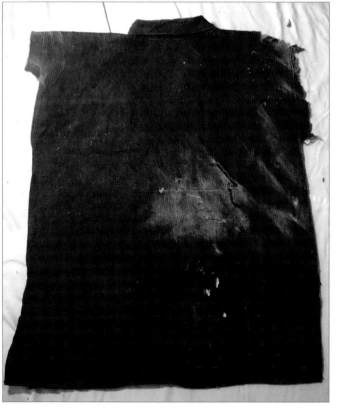

Back of the Greenebaum Brothers pullover.

The bottom edge is split at the sides.

Close-up of the breast pocket showing the leather "re-enforce laps" at the corners.

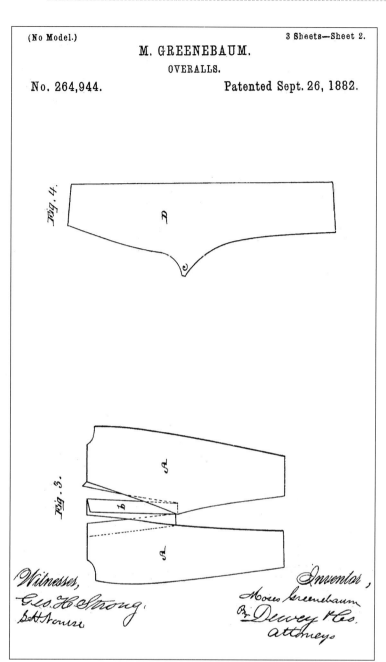

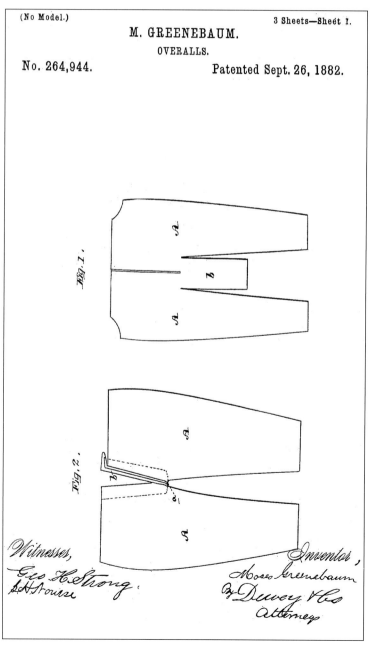

This 1882 patent is by Moses Greenebaum, who took over management of Greenebaum Brothers in 1879. This patent is for a crotch strengthening design. There was a need for a separate patent for crotch strengthening to compete with the riveted crotch of Levi Strauss & Co.

Neustadter Brothers

The firm of *Neustadter Brothers* was established in San Francisco in 1852 by the brothers Louis W. and Henry Neustadter. The business initially was located at the northeast corner of Battery and Sacramento streets. *Neustadter Brothers* was one of the earliest men's clothing manufacturer/dealers in San Francisco, and one of the most prolific. The company survived for approximately eighty years, and during its heyday was the best-known men's furnishing company in San Francisco.

Although Henry was a partner in the San Francisco operation, he continued living in New York City, where the brothers owned a clothing factory, until he relocated to San Francisco during the early 1860s. As was typical of early San Francisco businesses with eastern roots, the *Neustadter Brothers* initially sold goods brought in by ship. Their business during this period billed itself as "importers of gents' furnishings goods and Yankee notions". The firm moved its headquarters to the northwest corner of Battery and Pine streets at some point during 1866-67.

After his brief sojourn in the Far West, Henry returned to New York in 1868, and Louis left the company in 1872. Despite the departure of the founding partners, the *Neustadter Brothers Company* continued to prosper, albeit under new management. In 1875 Jacob H. Neustadter (pictured above), David Neustadter, and Joseph Rosenbaum became proprietors of the San Francisco business. Jacob Neustadter managed the business during the years they were competing with the *Levi Strauss & Co.* riveted work pants.

In addition to the transfer of ownership to the next generation of Neustadters, the company experienced two other major developments during 1875: the firm opened the *Standard Shirt Factory* on the southwest corner of Market and First streets; and David Neustadter was granted a patent for improved work pants. David was no newcomer to the business, having been a salesman with the firm since 1868. The name "Standard" had been trademarked by the company in 1874 and was applied to not only their shirts but, evidently, to the new pants designed by David Neustadter. The *Standard Shirt Factory* was relocated to Gough Street, between Grove and Hayes streets, during 1876 (this facility is shown in the following 1880 photograph).

Gough Street, between Grove and Hayes Streets, 1880.

The firm evolved continually throughout its existence. In 1878 Isaac Oppenheimer was brought in as a proprietor, and in 1883 Sigmund Feuchtwanger replaced Joseph Rosenbaum. By 1882, *Neustadter Brothers Company Standard Shirt Factory* was one of only two major manufacturers of men's furnishing goods in San Francisco – the other being *B & O Greenebaum Company's Steam Men's Furnishing Goods Factory*. In 1892, the company was cited as the largest manufacturer of men's furnishing goods on the Pacific Coast. The storerooms and showrooms alone filled up a five-story building. As the demand for greater workspace increased, the business offices were moved to the corner of Sansome and Pine streets in 1883.

The *Neustadter Brothers* company was best known during the late 1800s for their "Standard" shirt brand and their "Boss of the Road" overalls. An 1892 book extolling the virtues of the businesses in California commented, "No other firm on this [Pacific] Coast is so well known in the manufacturing of their special lines as this one is. From Vancouver to Mexico, a workman can hardly be found who will not acknowledge the superiority of the celebrated "Boss of the Road" overall, and equally well known 'Standard" shirts." The Boss of the Road brand may be considered improved rivetless work pants, even though, apparently, there is no patent for the design. So, Neustadter Brothers was selling two brands of strengthened work pants by the mid-1870s: the David Neustadter patented design (which will be hereafter referred to as "Neustadter jeans"), and the better-known "Boss of the Road" brand.

The Neustadter jeans design featured an extra piece of material sewn onto the inside top of the pockets, which (much like the Joseph Greenebaum design) could be applied to pants already made. The Neustadter design was the second patent granted for strengthened, non-riveted work pants, following the Jacob Davis rivet patent by almost two years. As the following illustrations demonstrate, an elaborate floral pattern was eventually sewn into the top part of the pockets to attach the extra piece of denim to the inside. The earliest examples of "Standard" pants have a very simple stitch pattern on the pocket tops.

The "Standard" brand name presumably was applied to these pants, as a suspender button on one of the surviving examples is embossed with it (see photograph). These "Standard" pants were probably discontinued in 1890, when the rivet became available for use by all pants makers. Furthermore, it is likely that they were never produced in great numbers, as the company's other brand, "Boss of the Road," enjoyed greater popularity and wider distribution. Very few examples of these unique pants are known to exist, further evidence of their limited production.

The history of the "Boss of the Road" brand before 1890 remains fragmentary, although riveted examples manufactured after 1890 are fairly common. The photographs include examples of non-riveted,

modified pants that likely were manufactured during the rivet patent protection period of 1873-1890. The strengthening improvement on these examples is a large triangular area of stitching at the pocket corners; however, no patent for this improvement has been found. Examples of other brands using triangular stitching have come to my attention recently. The *A. B. Elfelt & Co.* "Pioneer" brand, "The Montana," and "Golden Gate" all have the triangular stitching. These are pictured in other parts of the book. But, I am now unsure of the makers of the "Boss of the Road" examples pictured in this chapter.

There are numerous mentions of "Boss of the Road" overalls in accounts of the late 1850s in California, and at least one such account describes them as bib overalls. These pre-1873 "Boss of the Road" overalls most likely were manufactured on the East Coast as a bib overall for sale throughout the U.S., and may have been produced in a waist-pant version as well. They may have continued to be manufactured solely in New York as I have not seen a "Boss of the Road" label that has "San Francisco" written on it. There were other brands that used the triangular reinforcing stitching, so, the only way to identify a pair of unlabeled "Boss of the Road" jeans is if they have the patented (David Neustadter) one-piece fly.

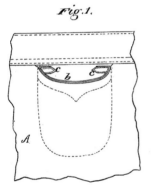

D. NEUSTADTER.
Fastening for Pockets.

No. 162,300. Patented April 20, 1875.

Fig.1.

Witnesses
Geo. H. Strong
Jno. L. Boone

Inventor
David Neustadter
by Dewey & Co.
Att'ys

UNITED STATES PATENT OFFICE.

DAVID NEUSTADTER, OF SAN FRANCISCO, CALIFORNIA.

IMPROVEMENT IN FASTENINGS FOR POCKETS.

Specification forming part of Letters Patent No. **162,300**, dated April 20, 1875; application filed March 8, 1875.

To all whom it may concern:

Be it known that I, DAVID NEUSTADTER, of San Francisco city and county, State of California, have invented an Improvement in Fastening the Corners of Pockets; and I do hereby declare the following description and accompanying drawings are sufficient to enable any person skilled in the art or science to which it most nearly appertains to make and use my said invention or improvement without further invention or experiment.

My invention relates to the manner of constructing pockets in clothing, so as to prevent their corners from being torn or ripped by an unusual strain.

To explain my invention, reference is had to the accompanying drawing forming a part of this specification, in which—

Figure 1 is a view of a section of cloth, showing my method of securing the pocket-corners.

Let A represent a pair of overalls or other article of wearing apparel.

In making the pockets in these articles of clothing, I take a strip, b, of cloth, leather, or other suitable strong fabric, which is two or three inches longer than the width of the pocket-opening. This strip b I then use to form an inside binding to the flap of the pocket, by sewing it on the inside edge of the flap. As the strip b is longer than the width of the pocket, it will be evident that its ends will overlap the flap at each corner of the pocket. These overlapping ends, marked c, I then turn inward and sew them to the material forming the back of the pocket, as shown, so that an unbroken or seamless corner is provided, the bend of the strip forming the corner. The seams of the pocket and adjacent seams I sew in the ordinary manner. By this means I provide a pocket-corner which cannot break down from unusual strain, as there is no seam to rip.

I am aware the pockets of overalls have been secured and strengthened at their angles by re-enforce laps composed of short pieces of textile fabric, extending across such angles at the points of juncture on the outside of the garment; but this is not my invention.

Having thus described my invention, what I claim, and desire to secure by Letters Patent, is—

A re-enforce for pockets in garments, consisting of the strap b, sewed to the inside of the flap of the pocket, and having its ends c bent inward and sewed to the back of the pocket, substantially as described, whereby the whole flap is strengthened, and at the same time the points of juncture are re-enforced, as specified.

In witness whereof, I hereunto set my hand and seal.

DAVID NEUSTADTER. [L. S.]

Witnesses:
GEO. H. STRONG,
JNO. L. BOONE.

For this patent, a reinforcing piece of material is fastened to the inside top of the pocket by a simple design stitch as shown. This simple fastening stitch was likely found to be insufficient and, in later manufactured pants was replaced by a more elaborate, floral stitch pattern.

This design incorporates an extra piece of material on the inside of a pocket top to reinforce the corners by folding the extended ends and sewing them to the material forming the back part of the pocket.

D. NEUSTADTER.
Overalls.

No. 196,693.   Patented Oct. 30, 1877.

Fig. 1

Fig. 2

Witnesses:
Edward C. Osborn
James McThompson

Inventor:
David Neustadter
By C. W. M. Smith
His Attorney.

The patents, such as David Neustadter's 1875 patent to strengthen the pocket corners of work pants, usually needed a second patent to strengthen the crotch area where Levi Strauss & Co. placed a rivet. The 1877 date of this patent can be used to date early examples of Neustadter Brothers pants.

This crotch-strengthening design is similar to that of Rodmond Gibbons, who is mentioned in this patent (see A. B. Elfelt & Co. chapter).

UNITED STATES PATENT OFFICE.

DAVID NEUSTADTER, OF SAN FRANCISCO, CALIFORNIA.

IMPROVEMENT IN OVERALLS.

Specification forming part of Letters Patent No. **196,693**, dated October 30, 1877; application filed October 28, 1876.

To all whom it may concern:

Be it known that I, DAVID NEUSTADTER, of the city and county of San Francisco, State of California, have invented an Improvement in Overalls, of which the following is a specification:

My invention relates to a certain improvement in overalls and pantaloons, having for its object to strengthen the garments at the point where the inner seams meet, where the greatest strain is received, and at the same time to simplify the construction and cost of manufacture.

To this end my invention consists in making the "fly" or facing of the sides of the front of the garment in one continuous strip or piece, and securing it in place on the edges of the front opening to the main portion of the garment, the said strip having the buttons of the fly on one side or half, and the button-holes in the other or opposite side, as will hereinafter more fully appear.

The following description of the nature and mode of applying and using my invention is sufficiently full and clear to enable any person skilled in the art to make and use the same, reference being had to the accompanying drawings, and the figures and letters of reference thereon, making part of this specification.

Figure 1 is a front view of the upper portion of a pair of overalls with the fly open and turned back. Fig. 2 is a view of the continuous fly separate from the garment.

The parts composing the overall A are cut out and united together in the usual manner; but instead of separate pieces being employed for the sides and facings of the fly, a continuous strip, B, is cut out lengthwise, or in the direction of the greatest strength of the material, and, after being doubled to form a finished edge on the front, it is secured to one side of the opening in the garment by a line of stitching, *a*, and to the inner face of the opposite side by the stitching *b*.

Thus the strip B forms, when in place, the front of one part of the fly, and the inside face containing the button-holes the other and opposite part, so that no other parts or pieces are required to complete this portion of the garment. It forms a continuous strengthening-facing, extending across the point of junction of the inside by seams, and it has the quality or property of resisting the strain thrown upon the weakest point of the garment, and of preventing any ripping or tearing of the material after a period of use and wear.

The buttons are secured to one part or end, and the button-holes are contained in the opposite part of the strip B, as shown in Fig. 2. They may be attached to and combined with these strips B before they are secured to the sides of the overall-fronts, and thus reduce the time and the number of manipulations required in the process of manufacturing these garments.

The use of this continuous fly-facing gives a smoother and better finish to the inside of the overall, and adds to the comfort of the wearer by removing the superfluity of cloth that accumulates at the junction of the inside by seams when the fly and the facings are cut out of separate pieces.

As thus applied and arranged, my invention gives greater strength to the overall without increasing the amount of material at the point to be strengthened, or adding to the labor of cutting out and making up the garment.

I am aware of the patent granted June 6, 1876, to R. Gibbons, and hereby disclaim the same; but,

Having thus fully described my invention, what I claim as new therein, and desire to secure by Letters Patent, is—

In overalls or pantaloons, the continuous strip B, extending the entire length of both sides of the fly, and secured thereto at every point, substantially as described and shown.

In witness whereof I have hereunto set my hand and seal this 18th day of October, 1876.

DAVID NEUSTADTER. [L. S.]

In presence of—
C. W. M. SMITH,
WILLIAM HARNEY.

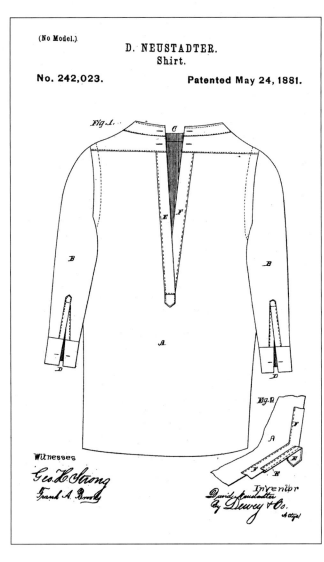

D. NEUSTADTER.
Shirt.

No. 242,023.   Patented May 24, 1881.

Fig. 1.

Fig. 2.

Witnesses
Geo. H. Strong
Frank A. Brooks

Inventor
David Neustadter
By Dewey & Co.
Attys

Neustadter Brothers, like several others, patented strengthening designs for shirts also.

Front of a pair of possibly Neustadter Brothers "Boss of the Road" denim waist overall work pants tentatively dated from the late 1870s to the 1880s. New information that I have received since this book was in the final stages, leads me to believe that any number of companies could have made these pants. The large triangular stitching was used by several companies in the late 1870s and 1880s. The very large patch on the right leg seems to have been used as a pocket.

UNITED STATES PATENT OFFICE.

DAVID NEUSTADTER, OF SAN FRANCISCO, CALIFORNIA.

SHIRT.

SPECIFICATION forming part of Letters Patent No. 242,023, dated May 24, 1881.

Application filed October 21, 1880. (No model.)

To all whom it may concern:

Be it known that I, DAVID NEUSTADTER, of the city and county of San Francisco, State of California, have invented an Improvement in Shirts; and I hereby declare the following to be a full, clear, and exact description thereof.

My invention relates to certain improvements in shirts and similar garments; and it consists in a certain combination of devices, as herein described and claimed.

Referring to the accompanying drawings for a more complete explanation of my invention, Figure 1 is a view of the back portion of a shirt, showing my invention applied to the back-opening and sleeves. Fig. 2 shows its application to the openings.

A is the body, and B the sleeve, of a shirt. C and D are respectively the back-opening and the sleeve-opening. These openings are very liable to be torn down as shirts are ordinarily constructed, and my invention is intended to strengthen these angles and prevent such a result. The back-opening is made by cutting a slit of sufficient length from the neck downward. A strip of cloth, E, is cut to fit over one edge of this slit, and is stitched to it so as to project upon the outside beyond the angle or end of the slit and overlap upon the other edge, as shown. This strip is stitched to the body of the shirt below the end of the opening, and extends a short distance below it, being also stitched across just at the end of the opening. Another strip, F, of material is formed, equal in length to the two sides of the opening. The center of this strip crosses the angle or end of the opening, and one side or half of it is stitched to the edge of the opening and to the strip E, so as to extend up on the inside of the strip E, the strip E having its edge folded over and stitched to it to give a finish. The strip F then crosses the bottom of the opening, as before stated, and extends up on the outside of the opposite edge, so that it forms a continuous strip across the bottom of the opening, and having a width equal to nearly the amount of overlap of the strip E. This gives a broad and strong re-enforce to this opening of the shirt, which effectually prevents it being torn down any farther.

In the construction of the sleeves the opening D is also formed with a similar strip at the bottom of the opening or slit, which extends up on the arm from the wrist-opening, and this is, in like manner, prevented from being torn down.

The formation and method of stitching the strips E and F so that the bight of the latter fits into the overlap of the former enables me to strengthen this part without an undue accumulation of cloth at the angle, and it presents a fine finish.

I am aware that it is not new to strengthen the back-openings of shirts by facings extending the entire length of said openings, and therefore I do not claim such as my invention.

Having thus described my invention, what I claim as new, and desire to secure by Letters Patent, is—

In a shirt having slits or openings C D in the body and sleeves, the overlapping strips E, stitched to one edge of the opening and across its lower end, in combination with the continuous strip F, stitched within the strip E, across the end of the opening and up on the opposite sides, so as to form a finish and re-enforce, substantially as shown and described.

In witness whereof I have hereunto set my hand.

DAVID NEUSTADTER.

Witnesses:
S. H. NOURSE,
FRANK A. BROOKS.

Front of a pair of possibly Neustadter Brothers "Boss of the Road" denim waist overall work pants tentatively dated from the late 1870s to the 1880s. New information that I have received since this book was in the final stages, leads me to believe that any number of companies could have made these pants. The large triangular stitching was used by several companies in the late 1870s and 1880s. The very large patch on the right leg seems to have been used as a pocket.

Close-up of the left front pocket area of the possible ca. late 1870s or 1880s "Boss of the Road" work pants showing the triangular stitching used to strengthen the pocket corners. This was not a patented feature. Note the similar strengthening design on the watch pocket corners to that of Rodmond Gibbon's 1876 patent (see A.B. Elfelt & Co. chapter).

Top of the front of the possible "Boss of the Road" pants.

Reinforcing piece of material
added to the crotch of the possible
"Boss of the Road" pants.

Close-up of the top back of the possible
"Boss of the Road" work pants showing
the shield pocket shape, the triangular
stitching at the pocket corners, and the
method of securing the attachment points
of the cinch strap by curving it up under
the waist band.

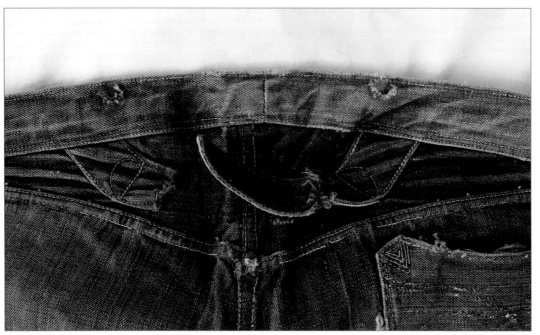

Back of the possible
"Boss of the Road"
pants.

Back of the possible "Boss of the Road" work pants.

Close-up of the right front pocket of a possibly 1880s "Boss of the Road" jeans. The stitching is quite sloppy. The decorative stitch on the pocket is a double line instead of the single line on the previous pair. Again, new information leads me to think that these were probably made by another company, other than Neustadter Brothers.

Top of the back of the possibly 1880s "Boss of the Road" jeans showing the right side of the cinch strap and buckle.

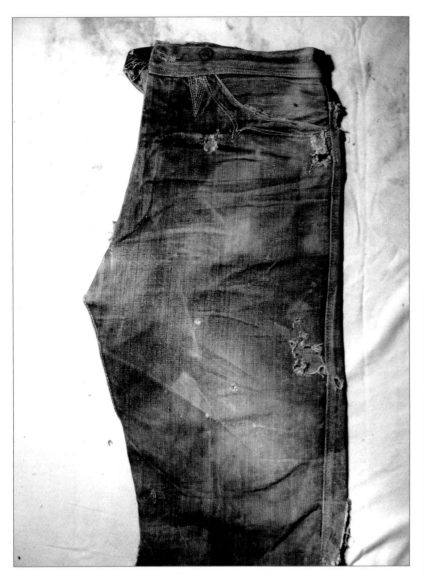

The right front side of the half pair of possible "Boss of the Road" ca. 1880s jeans.

Back of the half pair of the ca. 1880s possible "Boss of the Road" jeans.

Back pocket of the pair of Neustadter Brothers early(?) denim "Standard Pants." There is no decorative (floral) stitching on the top part of the pocket; that was put on later versions to secure the patented inside piece of material. (courtesy of Paul Andrews)

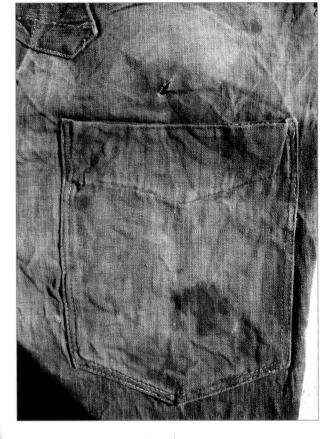

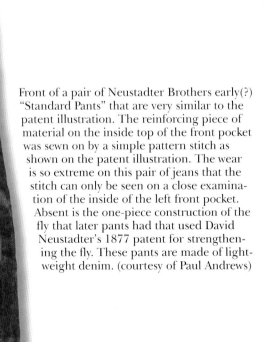

Front of a pair of Neustadter Brothers early(?) "Standard Pants" that are very similar to the patent illustration. The reinforcing piece of material on the inside top of the front pocket was sewn on by a simple pattern stitch as shown on the patent illustration. The wear is so extreme on this pair of jeans that the stitch can only be seen on a close examination of the inside of the left front pocket. Absent is the one-piece construction of the fly that later pants had that used David Neustadter's 1877 patent for strengthening the fly. These pants are made of lightweight denim. (courtesy of Paul Andrews)

Upper back of the early(?) "Standard Pants." There is no yoke. (courtesy of Paul Andrews)

On these early(?) "Standard Pants," the inside piece of reinforcing material on the back pocket has become separated from the pocket with wear. Adding extra stitching in the form of a floral pattern on later versions of Standard brand pants solved this problem. (courtesy of Paul Andrews)

Fragment of the left front pocket area of an improved Neustadter Brothers "Standard" denim work pants. The line drawing shows the points of the patent design by David Neustadter. Note the highly decorative stitching on the pocket top; this was an improvement to the earlier version that had a simple stitch used to secure the patented extra reinforcing strip to the inside of the pocket top.

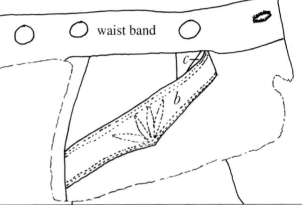

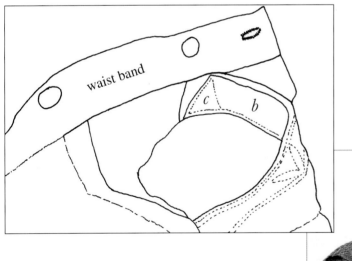

The left front pocket opened to show the reinforcing strip affixed to the inside top of the pocket and the end folded and sewn onto the area behind the pocket.

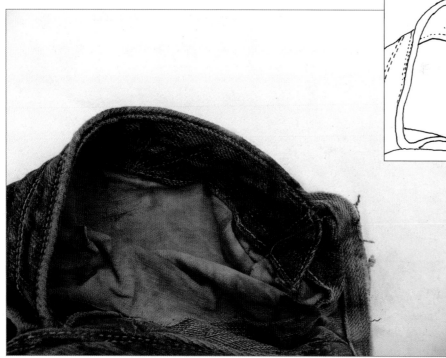

b: reinforcing strap sewn inside pocket
c: end of strap bent inward

The open left front pocket of a pair of Neustadter Brothers improved "Standard" brand work pants showing the patented reinforcement construction.

Close-up of a suspender button on the improved Neustadter Brothers "Standard" pants piece showing enough of a the word "STANDARD" to attach that brand name to these pants. Neustadter Brothers famous shirt brand was "Standard," which they made in their Standard Shirt Factory on Gough Street in San Francisco. Apparently that name was also given to the pants manufactured using David Neustadter's patent design.

The left front pocket tops of three improved Neustadter Brothers Standard Pants, shown together to illustrate the slightly different floral stitch patterns used to secure the patented inside strip of fabric. I am guessing that the oldest is the top pattern, with a full coverage to the edges of the pocket, and the middle is the youngest having the least coverage, with the edges brought nearly to points. The lowest pattern looks to be a simple rounding of the sharp corners of the oldest. I am postulating that all three of these were later developments of the first simple stitch pattern.

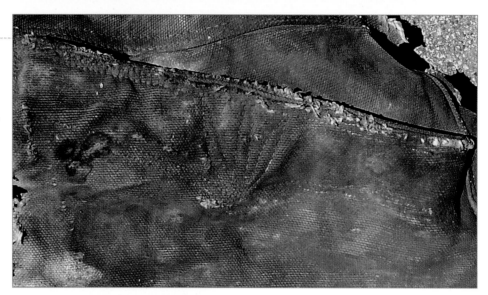

Front right pocket on a pair of Neustadter Brothers early(?) improved "Standard" duck pants.

Fragment of the left front of an improved Neustadter Brothers "Standard" brand duck pants, with the pocket stitching narrowed to the sides. I am guessing that this was the last improvement to the floral stitch pattern.

Close-up of the left front pocket of the "Standard" brand duck work pants.

Inside of the fragment of Neustadter Brothers "Standard Pants," showing the cotton pocket bags for both the watch pocket and large pocket.

Embossed suspender button on the latest(?) improved version of duck "Standard Pants" with the narrowed ends of the floral reinforcing stitching.

79

Right front side of a pair of improved Neustadter Brothers "Standard Pants" in duck.

Close-up of the right front pocket of the duck pair of Neustadter Brothers improved Standard brand pants.

The right back side of the duck pair of Neustadter Brothers improved "Standard Pants." There is no yoke.

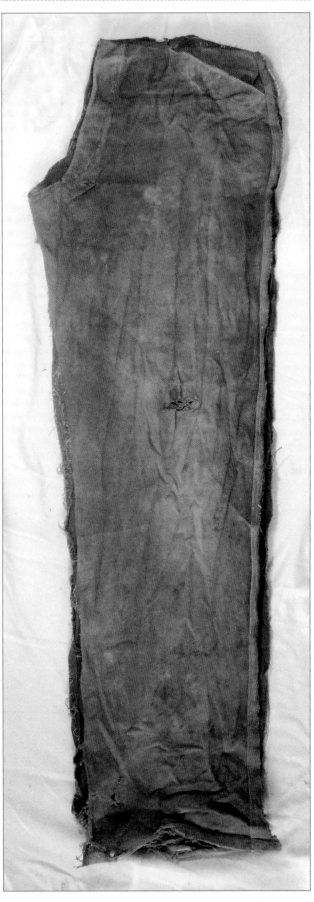

Full right side of the half pair of Neustadter Brothers improved "Standard Pants."

Samuel R. Krouse had a colorful twenty year career history in clothing manufacturing. His accomplishments are varied and include the achievement of two work-pant design patents in his name. Samuel is first listed in a San Francisco City directory in 1872, working as a laborer at the Pacific Rolling Mill. In 1875, the year his patent for an improvement in work pants was issued, he was a foreman at *Greenebaum Brothers*. In 1877, he was listed as a manufacturer of underclothing. The next year he was a foreman at *L. & M. Sachs & Co.*, importers and jobbers of dry goods, and worked there until 1883, except for 1880–the year his second patent was issued. That year he was listed under clothing manufacturers as "Krause Samuel R, 48 Second." That business may have failed, because he was again working for *L. & M. Sachs & Co.* in 1881. In 1884, he partnered with Moses M. Feder and was listed for two years as "Krouse & Feder, mnfrs clothing, 29 Battery." In 1886, he again was an independent manufacturer of wholesale clothing; but as a new address–111 Front Street. He remained an independent manufacturer of wholesale clothing until 1890 (the year riveting of pants became available to everyone) when he quit and took up work as a tailor and then again as a clothing manufacturer.

Since the year that Krouse got his first patent design in 1875, he was listed as being employed as a foreman at *Greenebaum Brothers*–already a manufacturer of improved work pants under their own patented design. I am surmising that Krouse's first patent design was manufactured by his employer. But, he stopped working for them the year after he got his patent, so the manufacturer is unclear at this point in time. Krouse then is listed as a manufacturer of underclothing and then a foreman for a dry goods importer (*L. & M. Sachs & Co.*). It wasn't until nine years after Krouse's first patent and four years after his second patent was granted that he went into gents' furnishing goods manufacturing under the name "Krouse and Feder." I am assuming that he manufactured jeans bearing his first patented design, but that is still unclear. Since I have seen a newspaper ad for that company stating that they were "Proprietors and Manufacturers of the Patent Stay and Self-Supporting Overalls, ..." The term "stay" is used in his first patent; so, this likely is an ad for overalls made with that design. (Daily Alta California, 5 July 1884)

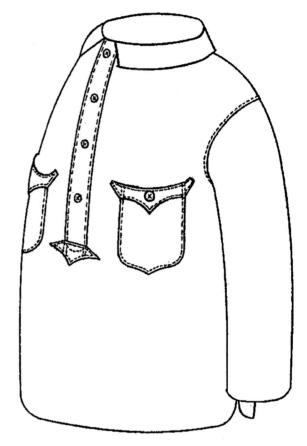

Inventor

Samuel R. Krouse

Krouse's second work-pant design patent of 1880 was assigned to the proprietors of *A. B. Elfelt & Co.* in San Francisco. Therefore, I assumed that they were manufacturing the known examples of this design.

The few examples that I have seen of Krouse's patented designs vary to some degree from the original design illustrated in the patents. His first 1875 patent illustrates and describes an extra piece of material added to the top of the front pockets. This is missing on the known examples. This may be explained by noting that the top corners of the front pockets were already reinforced with extra material in the design–a tab extending down from a button on the waistband and an extension of the rear cinch belt. Pants made using Krouse's first patented design are very rare.

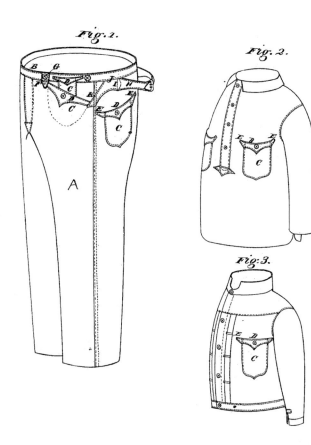

This is Samuel Krouse's first pocket strengthening patent for work pants. It is unclear who manufactured them. It may have been Greenebaum Brothers, whom he worked for at the time, or he may have manufactured them himself.

UNITED STATES PATENT OFFICE.

SAMUEL R. KROUSE, OF SAN FRANCISCO, CALIFORNIA.

IMPROVEMENT IN OVERALLS.

Specification forming part of Letters Patent No. **162,830**, dated May 4, 1875; application filed March 8, 1875.

To all whom it may concern:

Be it known that I, SAMUEL R. KROUSE, of San Francisco city and county, State of California, have invented an Improvement in the Manufacture of Overalls, Blouses, and other clothing; and I do hereby declare the following description and accompanying drawings are sufficient to enable any person skilled in the art or science to which it most nearly appertains to make and use my said invention or improvement without further invention or experiment.

The object of my invention is to provide certain improvements in the manufacture of clothing, such as overalls, blouses, and jumpers, and all that class of goods which are worn during manual labor, and are subjected to heavy strain at different points. These goods are very liable to rip and wear rapidly; and my invention consists in a novel construction, and the use of strengthening-pieces of peculiar construction at various points, so that I am enabled to counteract the greatest strain and overcome the tendency to rip.

Referring to the accompanying drawing for a more complete explanation of my invention, Figure 1 is a view of a pair of overalls made with my improvements. Figs. 2, 3, show the application to other garments.

A represents a pair of overalls, to which I have shown my invention as applied. B is the band around the top, to which suspender-buttons are sewed; and C C are various pockets. Across the tops of these pockets I form a stay, D, which is turned down and stitched to the upper part of the pocket, and resembles a flap or pocket-cover, without the use of the separate piece. The ends of this stay are carried out a short distance beyond the edge of the pocket, running to a point, and are firmly stitched, as shown at E.

By this construction I "tie together" the angle or juncture re-enforces, thus re-enforcing the re-enforces themselves, and at the same time protect the whole line of the pocket, and avoid the necessity of the ordinary pocket-flap.

In order to make a button-stay, and at the same time secure the band and pocket-opening, I make a piece, F, which is stitched with its upper end at the upper edge of the band B. The button G is sewed through this piece, and also the band, thus preventing it from being torn out. The strip F extends across the lower edge of the band, which is thus firmly secured. From this point it is tapered and crosses the corner of the pocket-opening, being firmly stitched, and forming a stay at this corner.

The back-strap H is so formed that it passes along from the point of stitching I, and its upper part beneath the lower edge of the band, as at J, and is there stitched in. From this point the strap extends downward and across the side or hip seam K, and the lower corner of the pocket C, thus serving as a pocket-stay and a powerful re-enforce to the hip-seam, which is thus prevented from ever ripping.

By my construction and method of strengthening the re-enforcing pieces I succeed in resisting the greatest strains.

I am aware that the angles or points of juncture of pockets in pants have been re-enforced and prevented from tearing by means of rivets, as shown in the patent granted to J. W. Davis, May 20, 1873; reissued March 16, 1875; and I am also aware that pockets of overalls have been re-enforced by small pieces of textile fabric sewed across the corners of such pockets, as shown in the patent to Greenebaum, August 25, 1874, and numbered 154,473; but such means I do not claim broadly.

Having thus described my invention, what I claim, and desire to secure by Letters Patent, is—

1. The stay D, stitched across the pocket-top to resemble a flap, and having its ends extended over and beyond the pocket-corners, to form the re-enforces E E, as and for the purpose herein described.

2. In combination with the waistband B, the compound re-enforce or stay F, when constructed and arranged substantially as and for the purpose described.

3. The back-strap H, constructed as described, in combination with the waistband B, hip-seam K, and pocket-corner, substantially as herein set forth.

In witness whereof I hereunto set my hand and seal.

SAMUEL R. KROUSE. [L. S.]

Witnesses:
GEO. H. STRONG,
JNO. L. BOONE.

Samuel Krouse claims that his unique design will "succeed in resisting the greatest strains." Krouse also mentions two other work pants strengthening patents that preceded his—J. W. Davis and [J.] Greenebaum.

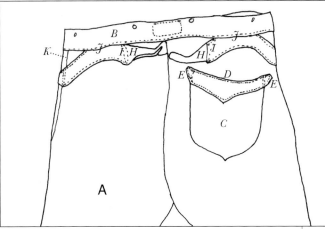

The back top of a pair of denim waist overall work pants manufactured using Samuel Krouse's 1875 patent. The cinch strap and the top of the back pocket are made according to the patent illustration. The accompanying line drawing identifies the parts described in the patent.

A : pair of overalls
B : band around the top (waist band)
C : various pockets
D : pocket stay
E : ends of the stay
F : piece to secure pocket opening
G : button (missing)
H : back-strap
I : point of stitching of back-strap
J : stitching of back-strap under the band around the top
K : side or hip seam

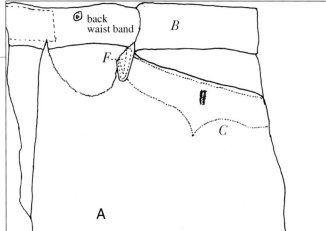

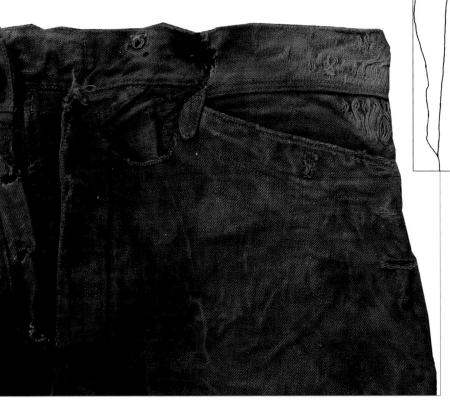

This photograph of the front right pocket of the pants shows that this manufactured example differs from the patent design in that the stay (D on patent illustration) was left off the top of the pocket.

Front of the pair of denim waist overall work pants made using Samuel Krouse's 1875 patent. This is how worn out a pair of work pants were before they were discarded. These jeans are dated ca. 1875.

The left front pocket area of Krouse's 1875 patent pants. The pocket stay (D) has been left on the watch pocket but not on the main pocket. Note that the piece of fabric (F) and the extension of the back-strap (H) serve to reinforce the pocket corners. The missing piece (D) would have been redundant.

84

S. R. KROUSE
Overalls.

No. 227,981.   Patented May 25, 1880.

Fig. 1

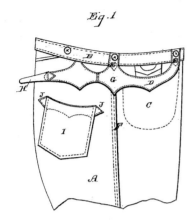

Fig. 2.

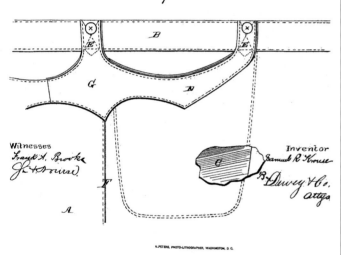

Witnesses
Frank A. Brooke
G. H. Krouse

Inventor
Samuel R. Krouse
B. Dewey & Co.
attys

N. PETERS, PHOTO-LITHOGRAPHER, WASHINGTON, D. C.

This is Samuel Krouse's second pants-strengthening patent granted in 1880. He is only one of two inventors with two such patents—the other was Yung Chow. The design of the one example I have seen is less elaborate than the patent.

Note that this second patent of Samuel Krouse's was assigned to Augustus B. Elfelt and others—the proprietors of A. B. Elfelt & Co. I assume, then, that A. B. Elfelt & Co. made the example pictured (the label is missing).

UNITED STATES PATENT OFFICE.

SAMUEL R. KROUSE, OF SAN FRANCISCO, CALIFORNIA, ASSIGNOR TO AUGUSTUS B. ELFELT, ALBERT A. LEVI, SOLOMON GOLDSMITH, AND ALFRED P. ELFELT, OF SAME PLACE.

OVERALLS.

SPECIFICATION forming part of Letters Patent No. 227,981, dated May 25, 1880.

Application filed December 27, 1879.

To all whom it may concern:

Be it known that I, SAMUEL R. KROUSE, of the city and county of San Francisco, and State of California, have invented an Improve-
5 ment in Overalls ; and I hereby declare the following to be a full, clear, and exact description thereof.

My invention relates to certain improvements in the manufacture of overalls and that
10 class of garments intended for outside wear; and it consists in an improved construction and application of strengthening-strips, stays, and re-enforce pieces, by which the body of the fabric, pocket-corners, and seams are strength-
15 ened, the parts are united to form a more complete mutual bond or support, while from their form a considerable economy of material is effected in the cutting of these parts.

Referring to the accompanying drawings for
20 a more complete explanation of my invention, Figure 1 is a view of my garment with the improved stay. Fig. 2 is an enlarged view of a portion, showing the inside pocket, &c.

The demand of miners, farm-hands, wood-
25 cutters, and other laborers for a stronger class of clothing has led to the manufacture of specially heavy goods for overalls, jumpers, &c., and many inventions have been patented for improvements in strengthening the pocket-
30 corners, seams, and other parts which are liable to be torn out by heavy strains. In some of these detached strips are secured across the pocket-corners and seams, while in others the pocket, waistband, and back straps are
35 formed in a single piece, which is stitched upon the outside of the garment proper.

In my invention, A is a pair of overalls, having the waistband B secured to the upper edge in the usual manner.
40 Instead of securing the pockets to the outside of the garment, as is frequently done with this class of goods, the front pockets, C, are stitched upon the inside, as shown, a proper opening being made at the top for the purpose
45 of allowing access to them. A re-enforcing strip, D, extends across the tops of each of these pockets, and is stitched thereto. The ends of this strip are carried up across the belt or waistband, there forming button-stays
50 E E. This strip is extended so as to cross the hip-seam F, and at this point it is carried

downward to a point at G, so as to provide a broad, and at the same time ornamental, re-enforce. The strip is continued back either in
55 one or more pieces, so as to form the back strap H. The watch-pocket K has a re-enforce, L, stitched to its upper edge to strengthen it, as shown. By this construction I form the re-enforce D for the pockets and the stays E
60 and hip-re-enforce G in one piece, but independent from the pocket or waistband, so that when stitched in place the thickness of the goods is doubled, and in some places trebled, thus adding considerably to the strength,
65 while the re-enforces are cut out with the greatest economy of material.

The back pocket I is stitched to the outside of the overalls, and the re-enforcing strip J, which extends along the top, is peculiarly at-
70 tached, being stitched along the inside of the pocket until it reaches the sides, where it passes between the pocket and the garment, and is thus brought to the outside, so that it is stitched along the inner upper edge of the
75 pocket, but has its ends stitched to the outside of the garment beyond the sides of the pocket. This makes a neat, strong, and serviceable re-enforce for this pocket.

I am aware that independent re-enforcing
80 strips have been employed to strengthen the corners of pockets, and that button-stays are made in the same manner. I am also aware that the pocket-stays and back strap have been formed in a single piece, and also that
85 the waistband, pocket re-enforce, and back strap have been made in one piece. I do not, therefore, claim these constructions; but

What I do claim as new, and desire to secure by Letters Patent, is—
90 The garment A, provided with an interior pocket, C, and pocket-opening, in combination with the separate re-enforce, cut as shown, forming the pocket re-enforce D, side-seam re-enforce G, and button-stays E, in one piece,
95 substantially as set forth.

In witness whereof I have hereunto set my hand.

S. R. KROUSE.

Witnesses:
S. H. NOURSE,
A. H. EVANS.

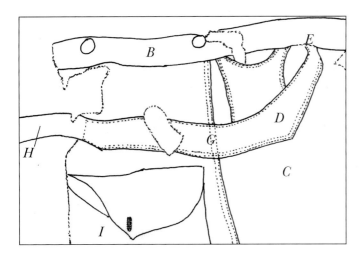

The top left side, front, and back, of a pair of waist overall duck work pants presumably made by A. B. Elfelt & Co. using Samuel Krouse's 1880 patent. Note that the design is simpler than the patent. There are two attachment points between the extended back-strap and the waistband that are left off this pair of pants. Instead of having two areas where the extended back-strap increases in width to join the waistband, the back-strap extension is nearly an evenly cut piece of material. Also, there is no "re-enforce" on the watch pocket as described in the patent.

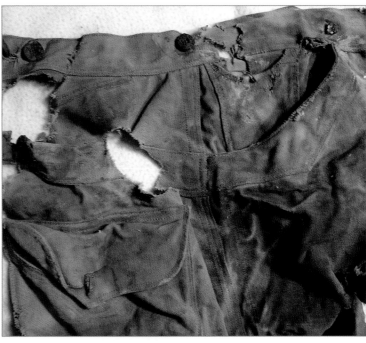

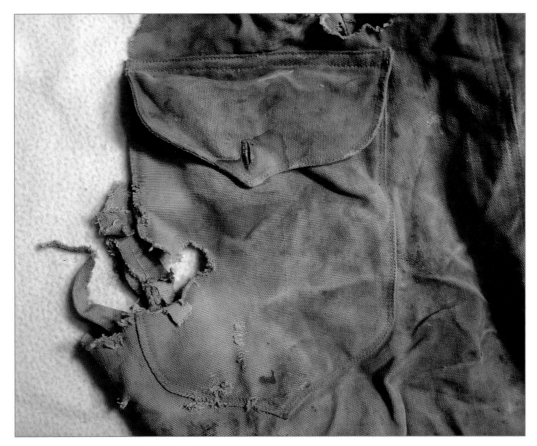

Close-up of the back pocket of the duck work pants made using Samuel Krouse's 1880 patent. No attempt was made to follow the patent design for the back pocket, which is very similar to his 1875 patent. A simple flap was used.

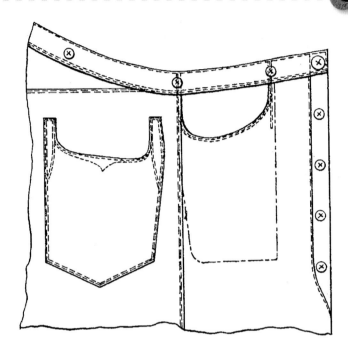

A.B. Elfelt & Company was established in San Francisco in 1867 by Augustus B. Elfelt, Albert A. Levi, Alfred P. Elfelt, and Solomon Goldsmith. Alfred Elfelt, Augustus's younger brother, and Solomon Goldsmith ran the business, while Augustus and Albert Levi ran the co-business of *Elfelt, Levi & Company* in New York.

I don't have a picture of Augustus Elfelt; but, on his 1866 passport application he is described as 5' 5" tall, with blue eyes and dark brown hair. He was born in Pennsylvania in 1831, the fifth of eight sons. In the late 1840s, several of his brothers had large dry goods businesses in Philadelphia, Pennsylvania, and St. Paul, Minnesota. Augustus left for San Francisco in 1851, and, from there, traveled to Portland, Oregon. By 1860, Augustus had been joined in Portland by three of his brothers and was working for *J. Kohn & Company*, a dry goods and general merchandise sales firm. He had also started a dry goods firm in San Francisco with David Weil–*Elfelt & Weil*. In 1864, Augustus, along with David Weil and Solomon Goldsmith, took over *J. Kohn & Co.* and named it *Elfelt, Weil & Company* (advertisement).

When *A.B. Elfelt & Co.* was founded in San Francisco, it was, along with the sister company in New York, set up to manufacture and sell clothing at wholesale. However, the business for the San Francisco firm was listed in the city directory as "importers and jobbers" of wholesale clothing and gents' furnishing goods. I assume, then, that the manufacturing was done by the New York firm of *Elfelt, Levi & Co.*

Then, in 1873, *A. B. Elfelt & Co.* reacted to the *Levi Strauss & Co.* debut of riveted work pants by producing their own riveted work pants–and promptly got sued by *Levi Strauss & Co.* for patent infringement. To compete with the riveted pants, *A. B. Elfelt & Co.*, bought the patent rights from Rodmond Gibbons for his nonriveted design for strengthened work pants. Gibbons had received a patent in June 1876 and had trademarked the name "Champion" for them in August 1876. *A. B. Elfelt & Co.* probably began manufacturing them in late 1876. It was reported in November of 1876 that they had forty-five Chinese and thirty-eight non-Chinese workers making clothing.

The firm secured the rights to another improved, non-riveted work pants design in 1880. Samuel R. Krouse assigned his second improved work pants patent to Augustus B. Elfelt, Albert A. Levi, Solomon Goldsmith, and Alfred P. Elfelt for a design similar to his first design patented in 1875.

The business partnership that had established *A. B. Elfelt & Co.* in San Francisco (and in Portland, Oregon, in 1881) and *Elfelt, Levi & Co.* in New York was dissolved in 1884. The business was listed as being in liquidation in 1887 and 1888. By 1890, Augustus Elfelt had reestablished the firm of *A. B. Elfelt & Co.* in New York.

Rodmond Gibbons, the inventor of the *A. B. Elfelt & Co.'s* "Champion Coveralls," had no other association with the company other than selling the patent rights to them. He had been the Dupont Powder Co. agent for gunpowder in San Francisco (advertisement) from 1861 to about 1870. He lived in Oakland, California, across the Bay from San Francisco, most of his life. Later in life, he promoted the idea of building a bridge across the Bay from Oakland to San Francisco.

He went so far as to have pilings driven into the bay mud off the Oakland waterfront. Some of them could still be seen in the 1920s.

The design patented by Rodmond Gibbons and given the brand name "Champion" was probably produced by *A. B. Elfelt & Co.* from about late 1876 to 1880. The "Champion" coveralls had the corners of the three large pockets–two front and one right-rear–and the small watch pocket all strengthened by elongating the corner-points vertically (photograph). One example is known with a cloth label on the back center of the waistband (photograph). Without this label, with *A. B. Elfelt & Co.* and the Gibbons patent number and "Champion" name on it, the manufacturer would not be known. As a note of interest, the label has the waist and length sizes inked on by hand. Examples of these pants are extremely scarce.

The second patented work-pants design by Samuel R. Krouse was manufactured by *A. B. Elfelt & Co.* beginning in about 1881. This second design had the back belt straps extended all the way around to reinforce the tops of the front pockets. Krouse's first patented design extended the back belt straps only as far as the outer corner of the front pockets, and had a second piece to reinforce the inner corners. (See S. R. Krouse chapter for details of these designs). Examples of Krouse's second patented design, made by *A. B. Elfelt and Co.*, are also extremely scarce.

Advertisement from an 1865 Portland, Oregon, city directory for Elfelt, Weil & Co., the parent company to A. B. Elfelt & Co. in San Francisco.

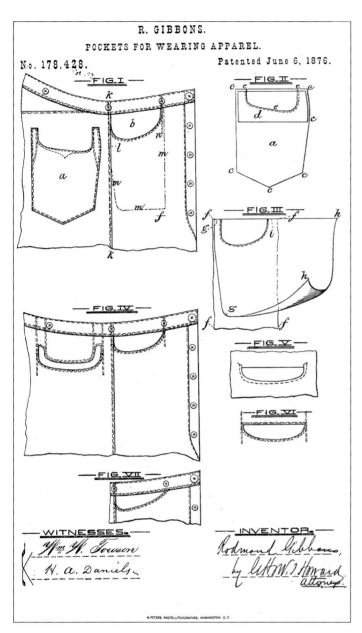

I know, from a pair of pants bearing a label, that this patent was used by A. B. Elfelt & Co.

Note that the patent illustration does not include a small watch pocket, nor is it mentioned in the description. The early example of the Neustadter Brothers "Boss of the Road" work pants pictured in the Neustadter Brothers chapter seems to have the small watch pocket constructed very similar to this Gibbons' patent. Gibbons may have been precluded from specifying the use of his pocket design for small watch pockets because of its earlier use by another company.

UNITED STATES PATENT OFFICE.

RODMOND GIBBONS, OF SAN FRANCISCO, CALIFORNIA.

IMPROVEMENT IN POCKETS FOR WEARING APPAREL.

Specification forming part of Letters Patent No. **178,428**, dated June 6, 1876; application filed May 25, 1876.

To all whom it may concern:

Be it known that I, RODMOND GIBBONS, of the city of San Francisco, in the State of California, have invented a new and useful Improvement in the Pockets of Wearing-Apparel, of which the following is a specification, reference being had to the accompanying drawing, forming a part hereof.

My invention consists of making a pocket for and in wearing-apparel, the opening of which pocket is without corners, curved upward to the perpendicular at both sides thereof, and stitched longitudinally in the direction of the strain to which said pocket is subjected in common use.

The objects of this invention are to avoid the transverse strain upon the stitching which should support a pocket; to dispense with cross-tacks, corner-patches, gussets, and metallic fastenings as pocket-supporters; and to secure strength and durability in pockets by a neat, simple, and cheap device.

The said improvement is applicable to and in the pockets of all articles of suitable wearing-apparel, and admits, without change in the nature of my invention, of various shapes and fashionings of pocket-openings.

To enable persons skilled in the art of manufacturing wearing-apparel to utilize the invention, I describe the same as follows, referring to the annexed drawing.

Figures 1 to 7 represent various forms of said improvement, and the modes of constructing the same.

In Fig. 1, *a* represents an outside pocket, and *b* an inside pocket, particularly adaptable to overalls, the dots in said figure indicating stitching. In Fig. 2 the manner of forming the outside or hip pocket is shown. The outside shape of the piece forming said pocket is seen at *c c c c c c*. By *d* is represented a smaller piece, laid face to face upon the other, the form of the pocket-opening having been marked upon it, as per dotted line. The two pieces are then stitched, as per said dotted line, and both thicknesses of stuff cut out, as per solid line *e e e*, say, a quarter of an inch from the seam. The piece *d* is then turned over and inward close upon said seam forming the rim of the pocket-opening, which is then stitched, as shown in Fig. 1. The

outer edges *c c c c c c* are then turned under, and the pocket is sewed upon the garment, as also shown in Fig. 1 by *a*.

Fig. 3 shows the detail of front pocket *b* in Fig. 1. By *f f f f* is represented a section of the right-side front *f* of the overall-pattern, as shown in Fig. 1. A piece of cloth, *g g h h*, is laid face to face upon the other, as in Fig. 2, except that the top edges of the two pieces should be even, the pattern of the pocket, indicated by the dotted lines, having been previously marked upon it, as in the other case. The sewing is then done as per said dotted line, the stuff cut out as before, the piece turned over and inward close upon the seam, and the rim stitched, as shown in Fig. 1. The piece *g g h h* is then folded at *i*, so that the edge *h h* shall be made to coincide with the edge *g g*, the fold thus forming the back face of pocket *b*, as shown in Fig. 1. There are two or more thicknesses of material brought together at *g g*, and in constructing the garment they are caught in the side seam *k k* as far down as *l*, from about which point the pocket is allowed to hang, as shown by the broken and dotted line marked *m*. A perpendicular line or lines of stitching are made downward to *n*, Fig. 1.

Figs. 4, 5, 6, and 7 are modifications in the shape of the pockets, the construction being substantially the same as that hereinbefore described. Figs. 5 and 6 show side pockets suited to coats, &c., the solid lines in Fig. 5 showing the cut in the cloth, and the dotted lines the pattern of the pocket-opening, and the first seam in the facing, as in the other cases. Fig. 6 shows the stitching of the finished pocket-opening, (shown incomplete in Fig. 5,) which may be made with or without lappet.

The greatest strain and wear and tear upon a pocket-opening are upon that side thereof upon which the hand bears the hardest when entering the pocket. Therefore, the purposes of this invention may be partially fulfilled by curving that side alone of the pocket-opening, as shown in Fig. 7; but I prefer to curve both sides, as hereinbefore described. The waistband, as seen in Fig. 1, overlaps, and the buttons are incidentally made additional supports to the pockets.

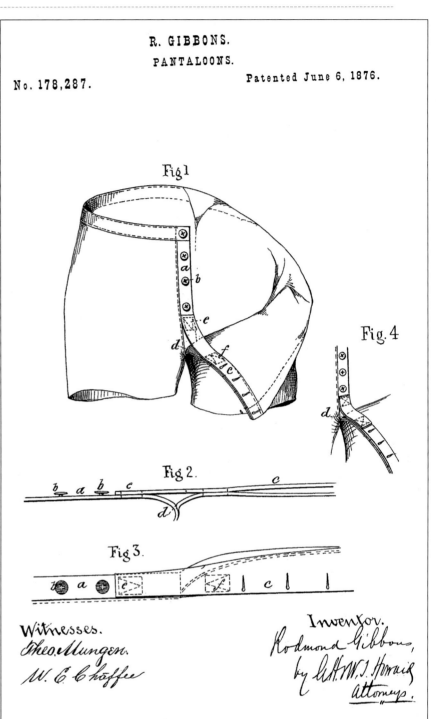

R. GIBBONS.

PANTALOONS.

No. 178,287.

Patented June 6, 1876.

A pair of A. B. Elfelt & Co. Champion Coveralls made to the Rodmond Gibbons patents. The missing leg may have rotted off due to acids or materials used by the workman wearing them in the late 1870s. I estimate that these pants were made about 1877.

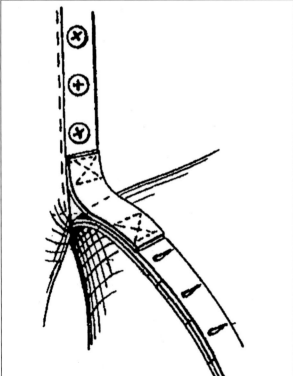

A close-up of the bottom of the fly of a pair of jeans that were made using Rodmond Gibbons' patented fly-strengthening design. The drawing is an enlargement from the patent illustration. Only one end of the patented strengthening piece remains.

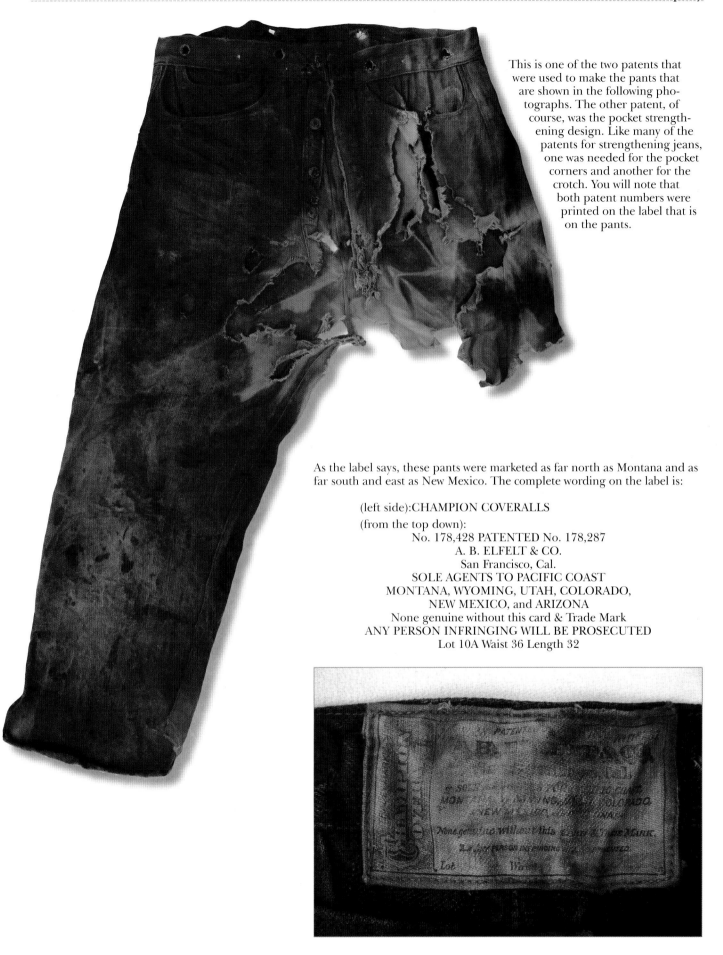

This is one of the two patents that were used to make the pants that are shown in the following photographs. The other patent, of course, was the pocket strengthening design. Like many of the patents for strengthening jeans, one was needed for the pocket corners and another for the crotch. You will note that both patent numbers were printed on the label that is on the pants.

As the label says, these pants were marketed as far north as Montana and as far south and east as New Mexico. The complete wording on the label is:

(left side):CHAMPION COVERALLS

(from the top down):
No. 178,428 PATENTED No. 178,287
A. B. ELFELT & CO.
San Francisco, Cal.
SOLE AGENTS TO PACIFIC COAST
MONTANA, WYOMING, UTAH, COLORADO,
NEW MEXICO, and ARIZONA
None genuine without this card & Trade Mark
ANY PERSON INFRINGING WILL BE PROSECUTED
Lot 10A Waist 36 Length 32

The cinch strap on the A. B. Elfelt & Co. improved Champion Coveralls. Note the larger size of the cinch strap attachments. Most work pants cinch straps were made large by the late 1870s, but this is by far the largest.

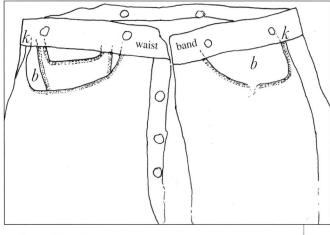

a : outside pocket
b : inside pocket
c : outside shape of pocket
e : cut of pocket
k : side seam

The front top of the improved version of Champion Coveralls made by A. B. Elfelt & Co. in about 1877.

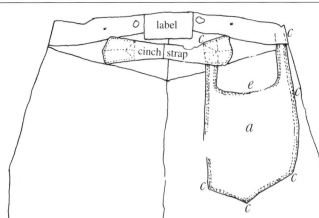

a : outside pocket
b : inside pocket
c : outside shape of pocket
e : cut of pocket
k : side seam

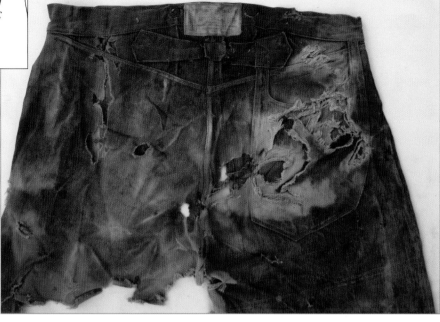

The back of the improved Champion Coveralls made by A. B. Elfelt & Co. in about 1877. Note that the construction of the back pocket differs from the patent design, in that one of the pocket extensions is sewn up under the cinch strap attachment.

Close-up of the left front pocket and watch pocket of the improved version of the Champion Coveralls made by A. B. Elfelt & Co. in about 1877.

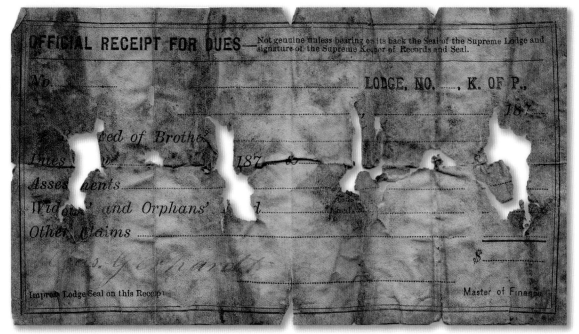

Sometimes things are found in the pockets of old work pants. This blank dues slip dated 1875 from a chapter of the Knights of Pythias was found in the watch pocket of the 1877 A. B. Elfelt & Co. Champion Coveralls.

A piece of a pair of denim waist overalls made by A. B. Elfelt & Co. ca. early 1880s. The strengthening design used at the front pocket corners is a large triangular stitch, which, I believe, was not patentable. (courtesy of Brit Eaton)

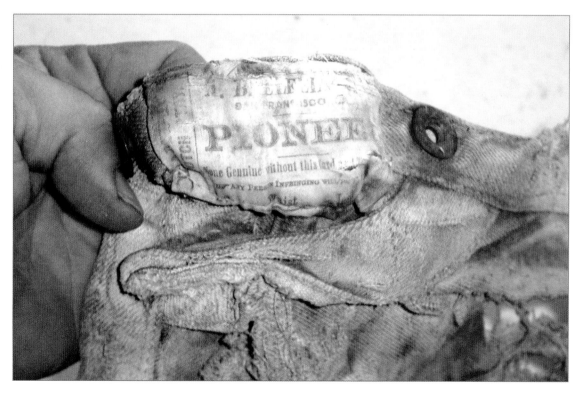

Label on the ca. early 1880s denim waist overalls. This Pioneer Brand was made before 1885 as A. B. Elfelt & Co. in San Francisco went out of business in 1884. (courtesy of Brit Eaton)

Close-up of a brass suspender button on the early(?) version of Champion Coveralls. These brass buttons were sewn on rather a steel shank button being used on the latter version.

Fragment of the back of an early(?) version of Champion Coveralls made true to the patent design, with a small cinch strap attachment and without the extended pocket corner sewn under the cinch strap attachment.

Fragment of the left front pocket on an early(?) version of Champion Coveralls.

Detail of the cinch strap stitching on the early(?) version. The small folded piece of denim on the left is the top of the extended left pocket corner.

The cinch strap on the early(?) Champion Coveralls (bottom) compared with the later(?) version (top). Note the increase in size of the attachment piece.

Some of the many patents granted to Rodmond Gibbons and an advertisement from an 1860s San Francisco City directory. He was the most prolific of the group of inventors that contributed to the designing of non-riveted work pants in the 1870s and '80s. Some of his early patents for gun improvements shown are presumably related to his gunpowder business in the 1860s, and may have been made for the Union Army during the Civil War (1863-65).
(continued on following page)

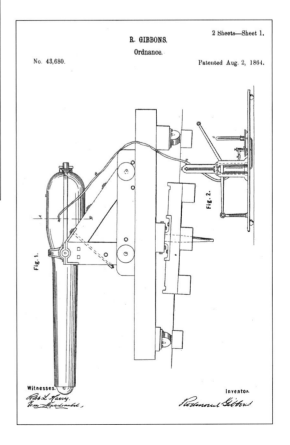

97

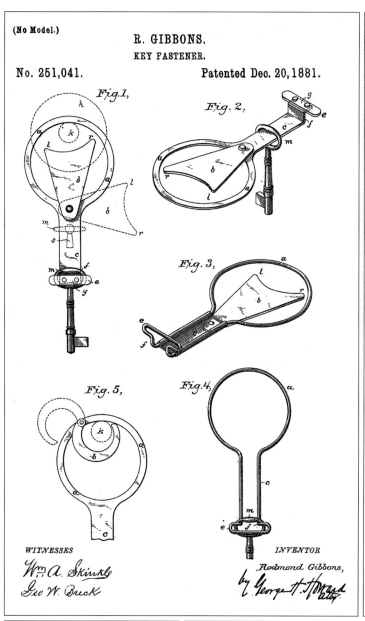

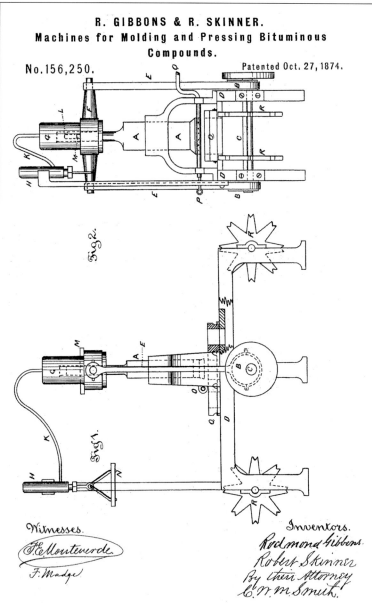

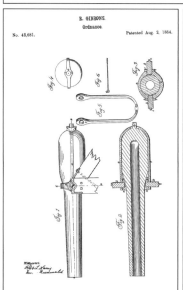

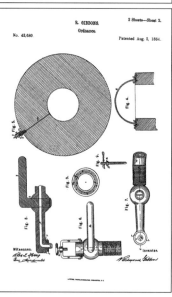

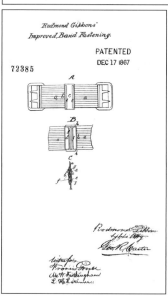

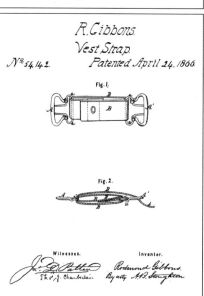

Heynemann & Company

Heynemann & Company was founded in San Francisco in 1861 or 1862 by Leonard Heynemann and Frederick P. Solomons. Leonard lived in England and would stay there, leaving others to manage the San Francisco firm until he left the business in 1881. The business was located at 311 and 313 California Street and imported dry goods. Hermann Heynemann came to San Francisco in 1862 to work for the company, probably as a salesman. In 1869, Hermann became a partner in the business. By then they had expanded to the importing and jobbing of dry goods, carpets, and upholstery, and were agents of the *Oakland Cotton Mills*.

The business was left to Hermann Heynemann and Frederick Solomons in 1881 and the name was changed to *H. Heynemann & Co.* until Hermann and Frederick quit in 1883. They were replaced by Manfred Heynemann (who had been working for the company as a salesman since 1873), Arthur Eloesser, and Emilio M Pissis, and the company returned to its original name of *Heynemann & Co.* Some years later the company became *Eloesser-Heynemann*, and *Eloesser-Heynemann* bought out their long-time San Francisco rival *Neustadter Brothers* in 1932. Finally, in 1946, *Eloesser-Heynemann* was bought out by *Lee*. Thus, through a complex series of buyouts and mergers, the resilient little company that started in the 1860s helped shape the modern jeans industry.

Like most of the other major competitors in the San Francisco workpants market, the Heynemann company reacted to the 1873 appearance of *Levi Strauss & Co.'s* riveted work pants by marketing its own version of strengthened pants. *Heynemann & Co.* trademarked the name "The Can't Bust 'Em" in 1879–an obvious reference to strengthened work pants–and Hermann Heynemann patented a strengthening improvement for the knees of work pants in 1881. But, to ascribe an improved work pants design to *Heynemann & Co.* that the company would have made prior to 1879 as an alternative to the riveted pants of *Levi Strauss & Co.*, some inferences have to be made. First, the company was probably manufacturing clothing in San Francisco in 1873. Second, their work force would very likely have included Chinese men. Third, the illustration for Hermann Heynemann's 1881 reinforced-knee patent

Inventor

Cheang Quan Wo

shows a pair of pants that also feature an improved pocket-strengthening design (patent illustration), which appears to be that of one Cheang Quan Wo. The latter inference is based on the observation that the design closely resembles the 1874 patent of Cheang Wo (patent illustration). Although there is no direct link between Cheang Wo and *Heynemann & Co.*, the striking similarity suggests that the "Can't Bust 'Em" work pants made during the 1870s and 1880s used the Wo patent. Nothing is known about Cheang Quan Wo other than his patent.

There is another possibility, however. A later, post-1900 pair of work pants with a label reading "Can't Bust 'Em" seems to be made using the patent design of Charles A. Jones. These pants are pictured in the chapter on Post-1890 Work Pants. The upper part of these duck work pants are made with an inner lining and the back pockets are formed by sewing the two layers together in pocket shapes. These features are the important design elements of the Jones patent. The Jones patent would have expired by the time these pants were made, but I see no reason for *Heynemann & Co.* to change the design of their most famous brand. So, there is a question about the patent design used by *Heynemann & Co.* for their most notable line of jeans. It may be, though, that *Heynemann & Co.* had two lines of work pants; one using the Wo patent and the "Can't Bust 'Em" brand using the Jones patent. This would be the same as *Neustadter Brothers* with their two lines of work pants and *A. B. Elfelt & Co.* with their two.

The patented design of Cheang Wo is very similar in appearance to the patent design of Jacob Greenebaum. The J. Greenebaum patent design adds triangular pieces over the top corners of the pockets and the adjacent seams. The C. Wo patent has triangular pieces attached to the side seam and the bottom waistband seam (patent illustration). In the known example, the triangular pieces are leather and they are sewn under the adjacent seams and over the corners (photograph). Examples of these pants are extremely scarce, making detailed comparisons difficult.

Looking down California Street toward the Bay in 1863. Heynemann & Co. was located on this street in San Francisco from its founding in 1861-2 until 1867, when it moved to 5 Sansome Street.

C. Q. W'
Overalls.

No. 157,902.

Patented Dec. 15, 1874.

Witnesses
John L. Boone
C. M. Richardson

Inventor
Cheang Quan Wo
by Dewey & Co
his Attys

THE GRAPHIC CO. PHOTO-LITH. 39 & 41 PARK PLACE, N.Y.

The design for this 1874 patent is similar to the design of the upper part of Hermann Heynemann's pants illustrated in his 1881 patent for reinforcement at the knees. I am making a speculative connection between this patent and Heynemann & Co. based on these similarities, but I have found nothing else to link them.

Wo's patent uses flaps of material, not separate sewed-on pieces like Jacob Greenebaum used to reinforce the stress points of the pants.

UNITED STATES PATENT OFFICE.

CHEANG QUAN WO, OF SAN FRANCISCO, CALIFORNIA.

IMPROVEMENT IN OVERALLS.

Specification forming part of Letters Patent No. **157,902**, dated December 15, 1874; application filed October 15, 1874.

To all whom it may concern:

Be it known that I, CHEANG QUAN WO, of San Francisco city and county, State of California, have invented Improvement in Overalls; and I do hereby declare the following description and accompanying drawings are sufficient to enable any person skilled in the art or science to which it most nearly appertains to make and use my said invention or improvement without further invention or experiment.

My improvement in overalls consists in forming a gusset or triangular lap upon the piece of goods which comes opposite the corner of the pocket or other termination of a seam, and then sewing the lap or gusset down across the seam, as more fully described in the following specification, in which reference is had to the accompanying drawing, which represents a pair of overalls with my improvement.

A represents a pair of overalls. In order to fasten the corners of the pocket and the termination of other seams in the overalls, I leave a triangular or other shaped piece of cloth, b, projecting from the piece of cloth opposite the corner of the pocket, and this small piece b I lap over the corner of the pocket or seam, and sew it down firmly all around, so that it will form a gusset for strengthening the corners of the pocket, and prevent them from ripping or being torn by any ordinary strain that may come upon them.

This piece b is formed in the proper place when cutting the cloth for the part, so that it forms a permanent part of one of the pieces of the overalls, and is, therefore, much stronger and more durable than if it were a separate piece sewed on over the seam. This form of fastening also gives the overalls a much neater and more durable appearance.

I am aware that seams have been re-enforced by sewing over them separate and independent pieces to prevent ripping, but this is not my invention. By my device the re-enforcing lap, instead of being a separate and independent piece of goods sewed to the garment, is a part and parcel of the body of the garment, and cut in one piece with it, thus not only avoiding the necessity of a separate re-enforcing piece, but also avoiding one seam, which would be necessary to secure a gusset as usually cut.

Having thus described my invention, what I claim, and desire to secure by Letters Patent, is—

A re-enforce for the corners of pockets in overalls, consisting of a lap-piece, b, being a part or portion of one of the pieces of cloth united by the seams forming the garment, substantially as described and shown.

CHEANG QUAN WO.

Witnesses:
JOHN L. BOONE,
C. M. RICHARDSON.

(No Model.)

H. HEYNEMANN.
OVERALLS.

No. 246,674.   Patented Sept. 6, 1881.

Fig. 1.   Fig. 2.

Witnesses
Geo. H. Strong.
Frank A. Brooks

Inventor
Hermann Heynemann
By Dewey & Co.
Attys

Notice on this illustration for Herman Heynemann's 1881 patent, that the pants depicted have triangular pieces of material covering the pocket corners. Only two patents had this feature–Jacob Greenebaum's and Cheang Quan Wo's. The difference between them was that the Greenebaum's triangular pieces were on top of the pocket corners and the adjacent seams; whereas the C. Wo triangles are under the adjacent seams or are part of the adjacent material. Depiction of the triangular pieces on the front pocket on the right in the above illustration is very similar to C. Wo's patent illustration. Notice also the similarity between the design stitch on the top part of the pocket and the example in the photograph.

Heynemann mentions in his patent the previous patent by Jacob Davis for knee reinforcement being for "use by persons of sedentary habits," meaning not strong enough for working men. These jean designers often found occasion to subtly slight each other's inventions in the text of their patents.

UNITED STATES PATENT OFFICE.

HERMANN HEYNEMANN, OF SAN FRANCISCO, CALIFORNIA.

OVERALLS.

SPECIFICATION forming part of Letters Patent No. 246,674, dated September 6, 1881.

Application filed May 17, 1881. (No model.)

To all whom it may concern:

Be it known that I, HERMANN HEYNEMANN, of the city and county of San Francisco, State of California, have invented an Improvement in Overalls; and I hereby declare the following to be a full, clear, and exact description thereof.

My invention relates to certain improvements in the construction of overalls and other garments for outside wear; and it consists in strengthening or re-enforcing and padding the knees, so as to make them more easy for the wearer in certain kinds of work, as will be more fully explained by reference to the accompanying drawings, in which—

Figure 1 is a view of my invention. Fig. 2 is a section view.

In many kinds of work, and more especially in mining in low tunnels and drifts, it is necessary for the workman to kneel upon the rocks or floor of the drift while using the pick and other tools, and this position, besides wearing the clothes rapidly at the knees, soon causes great pain and discomfort to the wearer.

My invention is intended to obviate this difficulty and protect the knees.

It consists in forming the knees B of the overalls A with a re-enforce of the same or of any other suitable or desirable material, which may be stitched on inside the main body of the overalls at the knees, and a quantity of cotton batting, wadding, or other soft material is introduced between the two thicknesses of material, and is then stitched or quilted firmly into place, so that in kneeling the wearer will always have a soft cushion to protect the knees. This re-enforce or cushion may be secured upon the outside as well as upon the inside, or upon both sides, if desired.

In some cases it may be found desirable to stitch a water-proof re-enforce upon the outside of the knees; but this will probably be found too expensive for the ordinary kinds of goods, and I therefore prefer to stitch the re-enforce upon the inside, as before described.

I am aware that a secondary piece of cloth has been secured to the knees of pants to prevent the bagging of the main cloth at that point, occasioned by their use by persons of sedentary habits, and such I do not claim, as such construction could not effect the purposes of my invention; but,

Having thus described my invention, what I claim as new, and desire to secure by Letters Patent, is—

As a new article of manufacture, overalls having the cloth on the inside, at the knees, provided with a secondary piece of cloth, between which and the body fabric, is secured a padding of wadding or other suitable material, substantially in the manner and for the purpose set forth.

In witness whereof I have hereunto set my hand.

HERMANN HEYNEMANN.

Witnesses:
W. P. COLEMAN,
HOLLAND SMITH.

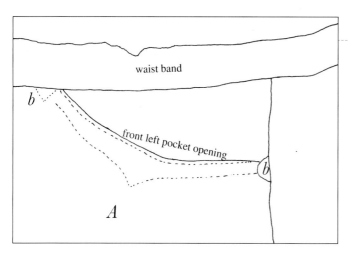

waist band

b

front left pocket opening

b

A

A : pair of overalls
b : strengthening gusset

The pocket corner reinforcement of these pants closely resembles both Wo's and Heynemann's patent illustrations. The leather triangles do not overlap the adjacent seams like the Greenebaum Brothers patent; they go into the seam. Also, note the design stitch on the pocket is the same as seen on the Heynemann knee reinforcement patent illustration. I propose that Heynemann & Co made these pants.

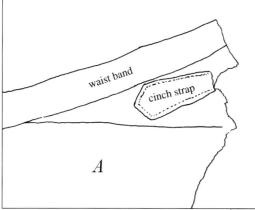

waist band

cinch strap

A

A : pair of overalls
b : strengthening gusset

Fragment of the left back of the pants that I propose were made by Heynemann & Co. This cinch strap appears to be rather "weak" in design, which is typical of the smaller cinch straps observed in examples from the early to mid-1870s. Most companies had larger cinch strap design and construction by the late 1870s.

B. & O. Greenebaum Company

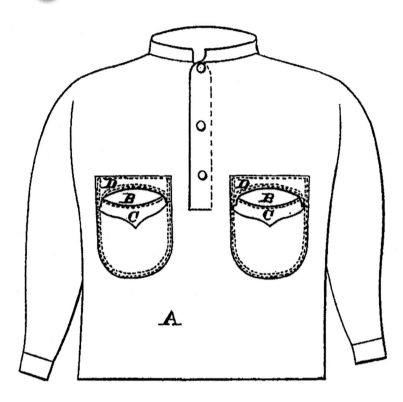

Inventor

Berthold Greenebaum

The B. & O. Greenebaum Company was formed by Berthold and Oscar Greenebaum in 1878. They were in the business of manufacturing men's furnishing goods, and set up the Steam Men's Furnishing Goods Factory at 23 Stevenson Street in San Francisco. Berthold had patented an improved work pants design in June of 1878 and trademarked the name "California" for "overalls, jumpers, and garments of outside wear" in May 1878.

The relationship between Berthold and Oscar is not known. If they were brothers then they were twins because they were the same age, thirty-seven, when they formed the business. They were both likely related to the Greenebaum family that founded the *Greenebaum Brothers* company. Berthold worked as a salesman for *Greenebaum Brothers* in 1869 and from 1875 to 1878. Oscar was working a few doors down from *Greenebaum & Brothers* in Sacramento and moved to San Francisco at the same time as Jacob and Herman Greenebaum, Founders of the *Greenebaum Brothers*.

In 1882 the *B. & O. Greenebaum Steam Men's Furnishing Goods Factory* was mentioned in a business publication as one of two factories in San Francisco manufacturing men's furnishing goods; the other was the *Neustadter Brothers Standard Shirt Factory*. The *Steam Men's Furnishing Goods Factory* had moved to 1047 and 1049 Market Street that year. The factory occupied two floors and employed 200 workers, 150 of which were women and girls. They manufactured goods worth 750,000 dollars a year. The word "steam" in the name of the factory meant that the sewing machines were all powered by steam. It was also mentioned that "large quantities of duck and denim goods" were being manufactured; but their main product was underwear. The firm closed in 1885. Berthold left the business the year before.

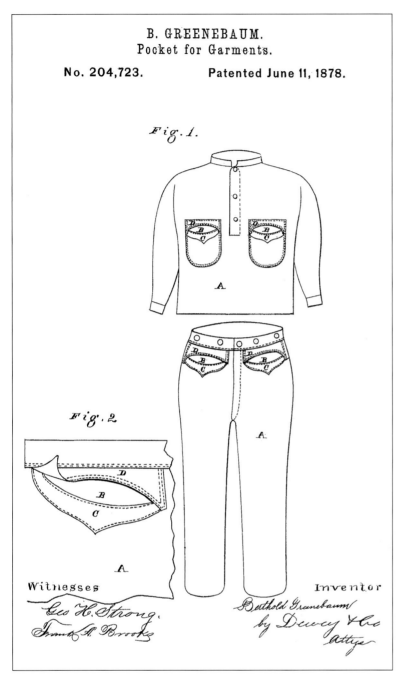

B. GREENEBAUM.
Pocket for Garments.

No. 204,723.   Patented June 11, 1878.

Fig. 1.

Fig. 2.

Witnesses   Inventor
Geo. H. Strong.   Berthold Greenebaum
Frank A. Brooks.   by Dewey & Co.
                                      Attys

This patent triple-layers the material on the pocket corners; much the same as Samuel Krauses' first patent in 1875 (but not used in the manufacturing of the examples I have seen).

UNITED STATES PATENT OFFICE.

BERTHOLD GREENEBAUM, OF SAN FRANCISCO, CALIFORNIA.

IMPROVEMENT IN POCKETS FOR GARMENTS.

Specification forming part of Letters Patent No. **204,723**, dated June 11, 1878; application filed May 16, 1878.

To all whom it may concern:

Be it known that I, BERTHOLD GREENE-BAUM, of the city and county of San Francisco, and State of California, have invented an Improved Pocket-Fastening for Garments; and I do hereby declare the following to be a full, clear, and exact description thereof, reference being had to the accompanying drawings.

My invention relates to an improvement in that class of garments known as "overalls," "jumpers," &c.; and consists mainly in strengthening the pocket-opening and the angles of the pockets by the employment of peculiar strengthening-bands, which are stitched, one along the lower and one along the upper edge of the pocket-opening, each extending past the other, and at the same time past the corner of the pocket-opening, so as to form a double supporting-stay or re-enforce, all as hereinafter described.

Referring to the accompanying drawings, Figure 1 shows my invention applied to jumpers and overalls. Fig. 2 is an enlarged view of the pocket with one corner turned up.

In the ordinary garments which miners, laborers, carpenters, &c., wear during their working hours, the strain brought on the several parts is much greater than on the clothing worn by business men. This is especially the case with the pockets, as weighty articles are so frequently carried in them, and the corners of the pockets usually give way first.

Various devices have been introduced to overcome this defect, many of them, however, adding an expense.

Garments of this class are usually made either of canvas or of coarse drilling, or similar material, and while they must be made strong, they must be made for a low price, and this my device enables me to accomplish, while the fastening is strong, and it is almost impossible to tear it away, because of the double diagonal nature of the fastening.

Referring to the accompanying drawings, let A represent the garment to which my improved fastening is to be attached. Around the lower edge of the pocket-opening B, and extending up past the corners on both sides, is secured, by a double row of stitching, the peculiarly-shaped binding-piece C, which may also be made of a double thickness of cloth, if desired.

Above the pocket-opening is another peculiarly-shaped strengthening-band, D, as shown, sewed all around its edge by a double row of stitching, and extending down on both sides past the angles of the pocket-corners, and over the end parts of the lower binding-piece C. Each part then extends diagonally past the other at the corners of the pockets, which they also cross diagonally, and each part forms a re-enforce or stay to the other, the greatest strength being at the point of greatest strain on the pocket.

As these bands are stitched through by lines of stitching parallel to their sides, the whole forms a strong system of diagonal stitching, which adds greatly to its strength.

In the case of pantaloons, the upper strengthening-bands D may be stitched under and to the waistband, and one side may be stitched with and to the side seam of the pants; and as the strengthening-band D crosses at each corner of the pocket past the other binding-piece C, it is impossible to tear away the corners of the pockets.

This method of strengthening the pockets is exceedingly simple and practical, making no material addition to the labor or cost of manufacture.

The corners of the pockets are thus supplemental with a number of thicknesses of cloth and diagonal stitching in addition to the cloth of the garment itself. This makes a strong, firm re-enforce or strengthening device, which may be applied to any pocket in the classes of garments for which it is specially intended, and which is neat in appearance and simple of manufacture.

Having thus described my invention, what I claim, and desire to secure by Letters Patent, is—

1. The bands C and D, stitched along the lower and upper edges of the pocket-opening, as shown, and strengthening these edges, respectively, said bands crossing the corners of the pocket-opening one above the other, so as to form a double re-enforce and stay, substantially as herein described.

2   **204,723**

2. The bands C and D, stitched continuously along the lower and upper edges of the pocket-opening, and crossing the corners of said opening and each other, as shown, in combination with the lines of stitching crossing each other diagonally at the said corners, substantially as herein described.

In witness whereof I have hereunto set my hand.

BERTHOLD GREENEBAUM.

Witnesses:
GEO. H. STRONG,
FRANK A. BROOKS.

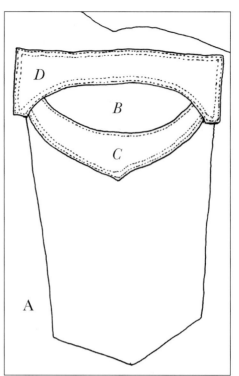

The back pocket of a B. & O. Greenebaum pair of denim work pants. The construction is similar to that shown in the patent illustration for a shirt pocket.

The cinch strap of the B. & O. Greenebaum jeans. The cinch strap attachments were strengthened by widening them and sewing the upper edge under the waistband.

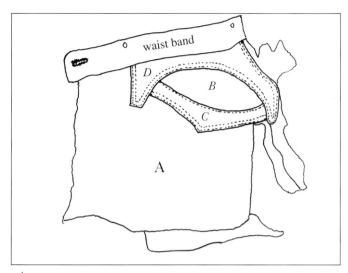

A: garment
B : pocket opening
C : peculiarly-shaped binding-piece
D : peculiarly-shaped strengthening-band

The right front pocket of a B. & O. Greenebaum pair of jeans. The construction closely follows the patent except that the right side of the upper strengthening band drops down farther to allow the pocket top to be angled down toward the side seam.

107

Harman Adams

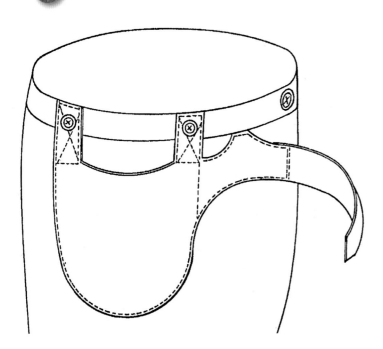

Inventor

Harman Adams

Harman Adams was born in Prussia in about 1818 and immigrated to the U.S. in about 1846 with his wife and first son. They lived in New York before moving to San Francisco. There, in 1876, Harman Adams patented a work pants design in which the front pockets and the back buckle strap are made of a single piece of material, sewn to the outside of the pants and secured to the waistband and suspender buttons (patent illustration). The name on the patent is Harman Adams. This is assumed to be the same as the directory listings for "Herman" Adams and "Hermann" Adams. Harman Adams is listed as having lived in San Francisco with his wife Rachiel and two sons in the 1860 U.S. Census. His occupation was listed as a tailor. In 1874, he was listed as a merchant tailor in Eureka, Nevada, but living at 235 Kearny Street in San Francisco.

There was no apparent change in Harman's financial condition in the years following his patent (1876), so he does not appear to have realized a significant gain from it. He moved to Bodie, California, in 1880 and continued working there as a tailor. There is no information on the use of his patent. There are no known examples of work pants using his patent.

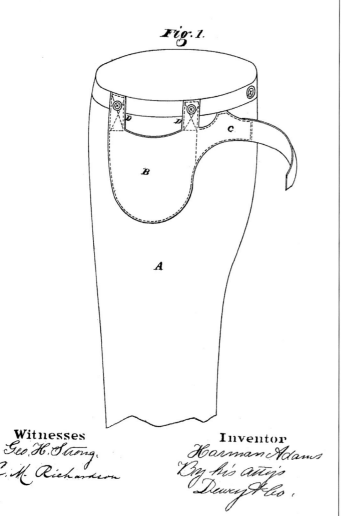

H. ADAMS.

PANTALOONS AND OVERALLS.

No. 173,433.   Patented Feb. 15, 1876.

Fig. 1.

Witnesses   Inventor
Geo. H. Strong,   Harman Adams
C. M. Richardson   By his atty's
                                 Dewey & Co.

This method of strengthening the front pocket and cinch strap is unique. Since no example of pants using his design were available for illustration in this book, the patent illustrations and wording is all that will be featured in this chapter.

Adam's patent claims these jeans would be easier and cheaper to manufacture due to the ease of cutting only two identical pieces of material for both pockets and cinch strap which would create less waste and require less thread than sewing several separate pieces on the pants.

UNITED STATES PATENT OFFICE.

HARMAN ADAMS, OF SAN FRANCISCO, CALIFORNIA.

IMPROVEMENT IN PANTALOONS AND OVERALLS.

Specification forming part of Letters Patent No. **173,433**, dated February 15, 1876; application filed July 7, 1875.

To all whom it may concern :

Be it known that I, HARMAN ADAMS, of San Francisco city and county, State of California, have invented an Improvement in **Pants and Overalls**; and I do hereby declare the following description and accompanying drawings are sufficient to enable any person skilled in the art or science to which it most nearly appertains to make and use my said invention or improvement without further invention or experiment.

The object of my invention is to provide certain improvements in the construction of pants or overalls; and it consists in the formation of a pocket which is sewed upon the outside of the article in one piece with the button-stays, which are above it and the back or buckle strap, and by this I save much expense of labor and thread which is expended in sewing on separate pieces.

Referring to the accompanying drawings for a more complete explanation of my invention, Figure 1 is a side elevation of my device.

A is a pair of pants or overalls, such as are ordinarily made for rough work. The pocket B is cut out and stitched upon the outside of the pants, as shown.

In order to save the time lost in applying and fitting the buckle-strap, button-stays, &c., when these are put on separately, as in the ordinary manner, I form my pocket B with an extension, C, at one side, and this extension serves as a back or buckle strap. Upon the top of the pocket I form two strips D, D, which extend up to the top of the waistband. These strips are for the purpose of strengthening the cloth at the point where the suspender-buttons are secured.

The pocket, being thus cut out, is laid upon the article in the proper position, and is stitched around its edges, the stitching being continued along the buckle-strap and also the two extensions D D, the whole operation being continuous.

By this construction I am enabled with the proper machinery to cut large quantities of these combined pockets, straps, and stays with but little waste of material, and when the stitching is done much time is saved, and the whole presents a neat and serviceable appearance.

Having thus described my invention, what I claim, and desire to secure by Letters Patent, is—

In a pair of pantaloons or overalls the piece B, having ears D D for button re-enforces, and extension C for a back-strap cut in a single piece, and stiched to the outside of pantaloons or overalls, for forming a pocket thereon, as described.

HARMAN ADAMS.

Witnesses:
GEO. H. STRONG,
C. M. RICHARDSON.

W. & I. Steinhart & Company

The firm of W. & I. Steinhart & Company was founded in San Francisco in 1859 by the brothers William and Israel Steinhart. Their company came to be known as one of the leading firms in the manufacturing of clothing on the West Coast and acquired two patents of early work-pant designs. They started out at 323 Sacramento Street in the business of importing gents' furnishing goods. William, pictured here, was born in Baden, Germany, in 1830 and had served an apprenticeship in the mercantile business before immigrating to the U.S. in 1848. Israel Steinhart ran the business in San Francisco while William resided in New York, where he managed a sister business with H. Heidelberg—Steinhart, *Heidelberg & Co.* In 1868 Israel also moved to New York and left their new business partner, Charles Adler, to run the company. Charles Adler had been a bookkeeper with *Levi Strauss & Co.* at 14 Battery Street when *W. & I. Steinhart* moved next door at 12 Battery Street in 1867.

Until 1872, the firm was listed solely as importers and jobbers of clothing and gents' furnishing goods, but in '72 they added clothing manufacturing to their line of business. In 1875, Samuel Scholle joined the firm as a principle and that same year Antonio Diaz Pena started working for the company as a stock clerk. The following year Antonio patented a design for improved work pants pockets, and, by 1878, he had become a superintendent at *W. & I. Steinhart & Co.* and was living at the Palace Hotel. It is presumed that *W.*

& I. Steinhart & Co. began manufacturing improved work pants using Antonio Pena's patented design. In 1882, Charles Adler patented an improvement in the crotch construction to the work pant design.

W. & I. Steinhart & Co. was still manufacturing and wholesaling gents' furnishing goods at 3-5 Battery Street in 1891 when the company was cited as a leading firm in the manufacturing of clothing on the West Coast. They had five traveling salesmen and a staff of sixteen operating the San Francisco office.

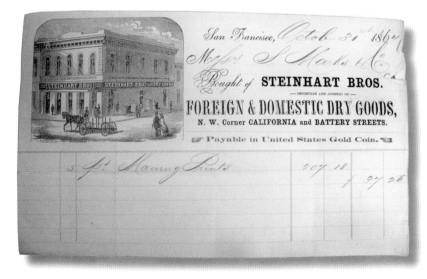

Steinhart Brothers was a dry goods business in San Francisco before W. & I. Steinhart & Co. I assume that the owners were related to William and Isaac Steinhart. Shown above is a receipt for a purchase made in 1864. (courtesy of the Judah L. Magnes Museum)

110

Advertisement for W. & I. Steinhart & Co. in an 1875 San Francisco City directory. Note the mention of the sister business in New York, which was Steinhart, Heidelberg & Co.

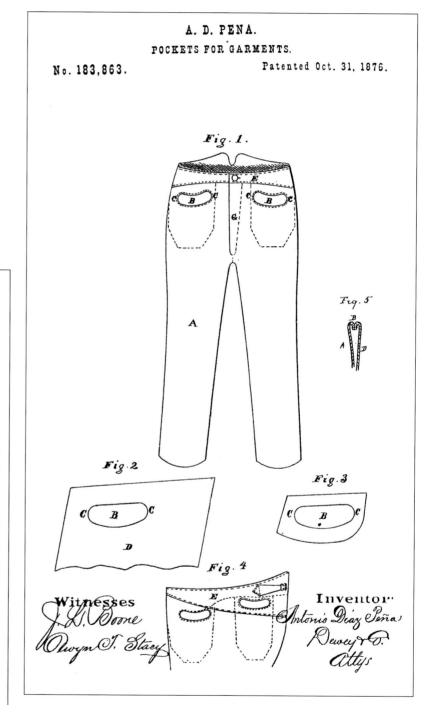

UNITED STATES PATENT OFFICE.

ANTONIO DIAZ PEÑA, OF SAN FRANCISCO, CALIFORNIA.

IMPROVEMENT IN POCKETS FOR GARMENTS.

Specification forming part of Letters Patent No. **183,863,** dated October 31, 1876; application filed September 19, 1876.

To all whom it may concern:

Be it known that I, ANTONIO DIAZ PEÑA, of city and county of San Francisco, California, have invented Improvements in Clothing; and I do hereby declare the following to be a full, clear, and exact description thereof, reference being had to the accompanying drawings.

My invention relates to improvements in clothing; and consists, more particularly, first, in an improved method of constructing the pockets of pants, coats, and vests; secondly, in an improved waistband for pants and overalls; and, thirdly, in the manner of cutting and applying the fly of the front opening of pants and overalls, all of my said improvements being intended to strengthen the parts and render the articles of clothing more durable.

Referring to the accompanying drawing, Figure 1 is a pair of overalls. Figs. 2 and 3 represent pieces of cloth with pocket-openings. Fig. 4 is a side view of top of pants, showing the form of yoke. Fig. 5 is a section from the edge of the pocket.

A represents a pair of pants or overalls. The first place at which a pocket gives way is the corner or angle at each end of the pocket-opening, because the strain upon the pocket concentrates at these two points, and, as pockets are usually made by uniting two or more pieces of cloth, the corners are only held together by stitches, or possibly by some patent fastening device, so that no substantial resistance is obtained except the limited portions of cloth held by the fastening device or stitches.

My improvement consists in forming the pockets without corners or angles to concentrate and receive the strain, consequently avoiding the necessity of using rivets or other re-enforcement for securing the corners.

To do this I cut or punch out the pocket-opening B, as represented, and the ends C C of this opening have rounding or circular lines, thus providing an oval or curved segmental opening. I then take another piece of cloth, D, and cut an opening in it which exactly corresponds with the pocket-opening B, and place it on the outside of the cloth in which the pocket-opening is made, so that the

openings will register with each other. I then stitch the edges together all around the opening, after which I turn the piece of cloth D through and to the inside of the pocket, and again stitch it down a short distance from the edge of the opening, thus providing four thicknesses of material. Any strain upon the pocket or lower edge of the opening will then be received by the strength of four thicknesses of cloth along the entire rounded or circular portion at each end of the pocket, thus giving ample strength of material to resist any ordinary strain that may come upon the pocket.

Instead of an ordinary waist-band, as usually employed in the manufacture of pants, I construct a yoke, E, which extends from the front around upon each side of the pants to the back, where the two yokes are united. Each yoke extends downward and backward and is made in a single piece of goods, thus obviating the necessity of piecing out the portion around the pockets, and as it widens toward the back it gives the wearer greater comfort and a better fit.

I thus provide valuable improvements in clothing, and at the same time simplify their manufacture.

Having thus described my invention, what I claim, and desire to secure by Letters Patent, is—

1. A garment provided with elongated pocket-opening, cut out of its main body and having rounded ends, as set forth.

2. The method of re-enforcing pockets, consisting in laying on the outside of the garment a re-enforce, D, having an opening coinciding with the pocket-opening, stitching the two together around the edge of the pocket opening, and then turning the re-enforce through the pocket-opening to the inside, and stitching down with one or more rows of stitches, as set forth.

3. The yoke waistband E, gradually widened from front to rear, substantially as described.

In witness whereof I have hereunto set my hand and seal.

ANTONIO DIAZ PEÑA. [L. S.]

Witnesses:
OLWYN T. STACY,
FRANK A. BROOKS.

The Pena pocket design is quite distinctive, featuring an oval opening cut in the pants for a pocket. In examples, I have only found this pocket design used for back pockets, not front pockets.

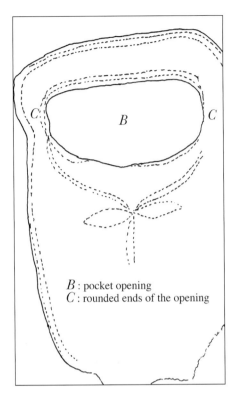

The left back pocket of a pair of denim waist overall work pants made with Pena's patent design. The "floral" design on the pocket is similar to the Neustadter Brothers' design stitch on their rear pocket. I assume that these jeans were made by W. & I. Steinhart & Co. because of their close association with Antonio Pena.

B : pocket opening
C : rounded ends of the opening

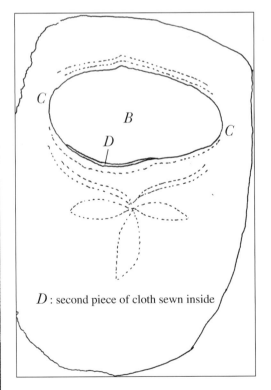

D : second piece of cloth sewn inside

The right back pocket of the same pair of denim work pants. The construction differs from the patent design in that the pocket is made of two pieces of material sewn on the outside of the pants instead of one piece sewn on the inside.

Toklas, Brown & Company

Toklas, Brown & Co., founded in San Francisco in 1876, was the fourth clothing import company formed by Max Toklas with a succession of different partners, starting in 1864. The first was *Toklas M. & Company* started by Max Toklas, Soloman Sheyer, and L. Lithauer. The next year L. Lithauer was replaced by Morris Wise and the company was renamed *Toklas, Wise & Company*. In 1868 Soloman Sheyer was replaced by Seligman Hahn and in 1871, Morris Wise was replaced by Morris Brown and the company was renamed *Toklas, Hahn and Brown*. Max Toklas moved to New York in 1871, apparently leaving his son Ferdinand Toklas to take care of his interests in San Francisco. The Toklas clothing companies came to an end in San Francisco in 1880. But, by that time Ferdinand Toklas had set up several other clothing firms in Oregon and Washington Territory–*Toklas & Singerman* in Seattle became an important retail store in the twentieth century. As a side note, Ferdinand Toklas was the father of Alice B. Toklas who came to fame during her association with Gertrude Stein, the celebrated author.

The Toklas companies had been manufacturing clothing in San Francisco since 1868; however, their response to the debut of the riveted work pants of *Levi Strauss & Co.* in 1873 apparently took a few years. In November 1877, Leon Aronson was granted a patent for improved work pants that was assigned to *Toklas, Brown & Co.* (patent). Leon Aronson was working as a salesman for *Brown Brothers* at the time, a company closely associated with *Toklas, Brown & Co.* In fact, *Brown Brothers* seems to have assumed the business of *Toklas, Brown & Co.* when the latter quit the clothing business in San Francisco in 1880. In 1881, *Brown Brothers* began manufacturing mens' furnishing goods at the same address vacated by *Toklas, Brown & Co.* Leon Aronson is last listed in the San Francisco City directory as a salesman for Brown Brothers in 1882.

Little is known about Leon Aronson other than he was born in Russia in about 1830, and that he was in the clothing business in Sacramento in 1870. I assume that Leon Aronson's patented design for improved work pants was used by *Toklas, Brown & Co.* starting in about 1878, and possibly later by *Brown Brothers*.

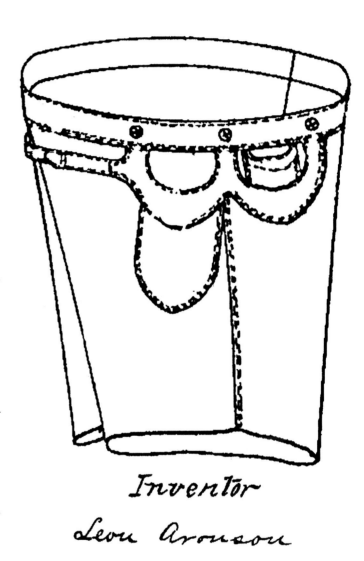

Inventor

Leon Aronson

The article in an 1889 issue of the *Daily Alta California* about Brown Brothers mentions one of their special brands as "... Golden Gate Overalls." This may have been their brand name for the Aronson patent designed work pants. The patent design uses a single piece (or two pieces) of material to form the waist band, the buckle straps, and three loops to be sewn in place as pocket tops or stays (patent illustration). No examples of work pants made using this patent are known to exist.

Label on a suit jacket made
by Toklas, Brown & Co.
(courtesy of Mike Hodis)

An advertisement for Toklas, Hahn & Brown,
the predecessor company to Toklas, Brown &
Co. in San Francisco. The ad is from The Hebrew, a San Francisco newspaper. (courtesy of
the Judah L. Magnes Museum)

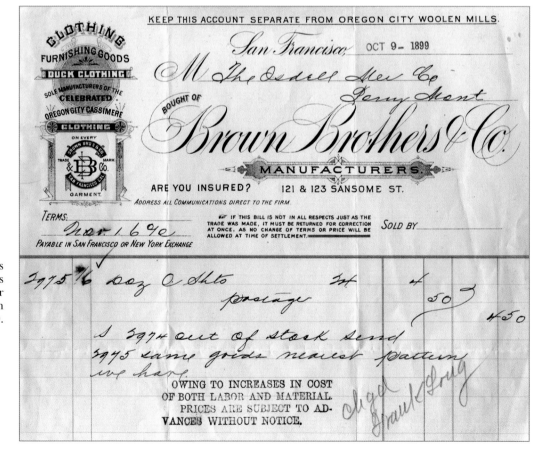

A bill from Brown Brothers
from 1899. Brown Brothers
appears to have taken over
the clothing business from
Toklas Brown & Co. in 1880.
(courtesy of Mike Hodis)

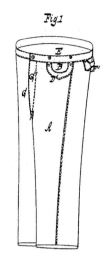

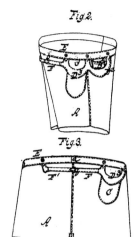

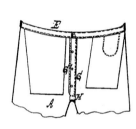

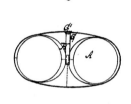

L. ARONSON.
Overalls.

No. 196,856.   Patented Nov. 6, 1877.

Fig.1   Fig.2

Fig.3

Fig.4   Fig.5

Witnesses.
Otto Hufland
Chas Wallers.

Inventor
Leon Aronson   by
Van Santvoord & Hauff
his attorneys

I believe that I have seen a fragment of jeans made using this patent design, but I have no record of it.

The strength of the pockets and cinch strap were increased by cutting a single intricate waistband to include all of the parts in one piece as shown in the patent illustration.

UNITED STATES PATENT OFFICE.

LEON ARONSON, OF SAN FRANCISCO, CALIFORNIA, ASSIGNOR TO TOKLAS, BROWN & CO., OF NEW YORK, N. Y.

IMPROVEMENT IN OVERALLS.

Specification forming part of Letters Patent No. **196,856,** dated November 6, 1877; application filed August 15, 1877.

To all whom it may concern:

Be it known that I, LEON ARONSON, of the city and county of San Francisco, and State of California, have invented a new and useful Improvement in Overalls, which invention is fully described in the following specification, reference being had to the accompanying drawing, forming part of this specification, in which drawing—

Figure 1 represents a side elevation of a pair of overalls containing my improvement. Fig. 2 is a like view, looking in an opposite direction to Fig. 1. Fig. 3 is a rear view of the same. Fig. 4 is a vertical section thereof, looking toward the front of the article. Fig. 5 is a horizontal section of the same.

Similar letters indicate corresponding parts.

My improvement relates to the construction of overalls or pants; and has for its object to strengthen those parts thereof which are subjected to heavy strain, and to accomplish this purpose without materially increasing the cost of the article, if at all.

It consists in a waistband having facings or stays for a rear pocket and for the front pockets of the overalls, and having a buckle strap or straps, all cut out in one piece with such band, the facings or stays being stitched to the outer edges of said pockets, so that the latter are rendered capable of resisting a great amount of strain, while said facings or stays, as well as the buckle strap or straps, by being made in one piece with said waistband, are not only rendered exceedingly strong and durable, but can be produced with comparatively very little labor.

In the drawing, the letter A designates a pair of overalls, having pockets B B' on the opposite and front parts thereof, and having a rear pocket, C. These pockets are, respectively, provided with facings or stays D¹ D² D³, which are stitched around the outer or free edges thereof, and cut out to the proper shape in one piece with the waistband E.

In the example shown, the waistband E is made in two parts, and united on the rear part of the overalls, as at *a*, the front pocket B and the rear pocket C being formed with one half or part of said waistband, while the other front pocket, B', is formed with the other part thereof; but, if desired, the waistband E can be formed of a single or undivided piece.

On the rear part of the overalls are located two buckle-straps, F F', one of which is provided with a buckle, *b*. Each of these straps F F' is cut out in one piece with the waistband E, and with the facings of the several pockets B, B', and C, the strap F being made to extend from the facing D³ of the rear pocket C, while the strap F extends directly from the waistband.

It will be seen that by the above construction great strength is given to the pockets of the overalls at the points where the same are subjected to heavy strain, while little or no time is lost in applying either the pocket-facings or the buckle-straps, the greatest possible strength and durability being, moreover, given to said facings and straps, and comparatively little labor being involved in their production.

My overalls have the usual opening in their front part, the edges G G' of which lap over each other, and the inner lap G is provided with an extension, H. (See Figs. 4 and 5.) This extension H is stitched over the seams at the crotch, on the inside of the overalls, and by its means such seams are, to a great extent, re-enforced.

I am aware of the patent to S. R. Krouse, dated May 4, 1875, No. 162,830; but as I do not employ the construction and arrangement therein shown, the same is hereby disclaimed.

What I claim as new, and desire to secure by Letters Patent, is—

As a new article of manufacture, the overalls or pants herein described, having the waistband, buckle-straps, and front and rear pocket-facings cut in one piece.

In testimony that I claim the foregoing I have hereunto set my hand and seal this 11th day of July, 1877.

LEON ARONSON. [L. S.]

Witnesses:
FERDINAND TOKLAS,
S. H. BARNHISEL.

William G. Badger & Company

William G. Badger and the company *Badger & Lindenberger* (Thomas E.) were listed as being in San Francisco in 1861. The firm's business was importing and jobbing of clothing and other goods, and they were agents for Chickering & Son's piano-fortes. The address was 411, 413, and 415 Battery Street. William Badger was born in Charlestown, Massachusetts, in 1821 and had arrived in San Francisco in 1850.

William moved to Fruit Vale, across the Bay in Alameda County, in 1871. The business was moved to 7 Sansom Street, and the name was changed to *William G. Badger*, as Lindenberger was no longer a partner. William continued running the business by himself during the mid-1870s, operating as a commission merchant and a seller of pianos and organs. In 1877, he added a partner named Charles Underwood and changed the firm's name to *William G. Badger & Company*. By the next year they were manufacturing clothing and selling wholesale furnishing goods. About the same time, he trademarked the name "Hercules" for "overalls, jumpers, and ready-made goods for outside wear." This suggests that they were making and selling an improved work overall, in competition with the other San Francisco work-pants manufacturers. There is no patent on record for either William Badger or Charles Underwood for a strengthening improvement to work pants. However, Charles was an inventor with at least two patents for clothing improvements, and he might have been brought into the company for his invention of an improved work pants design, one that never was granted a patent. The partnership was dissolved by 1879, and the company name returned to *William G. Badger*. He is last listed as a clothing manufacturer or wholesaler, in 1886. His firm did thrive and become a large mercantile business by 1892. There is no information on the kind of improved work pants the company may have produced prior to 1890, but the name "Hercules" was used for most of the first half of the twentieth century as a brand for riveted work pants sold through the *Sears and Roebuck Co.* I have seen catalogues from the 1930s with the brand advertised as being made on the West Coast – presumably, San Francisco.

Meyerstein & Lowenberg

Lewis Meyerstein and Isidor Lowenberg were business associates, and (perhaps) relatives. Isidor was born in Prussia in about 1835, and immigrated to the U.S. in 1853. Lewis was born in Prussia in about 1829, and came to the U.S. when he was a young man. Their wives were both born in Alabama to Prussian and Bavarian parents. By 1861, they were in the retail clothing business in San Francisco as *Meyerstein & Lowenberg*, and residing at their business address–the northwest corner of Bush and Kearny streets. Throughout the 1860s they lived close to each other, ending up on Van Ness Avenue as neighbors in 1869.

Their retail clothing business thrived without much change until they added clothing manufacturing in 1877. The business then was moved to 25 Sansome Street, presumably to accommodate the manufacturing, and to 109 Sansome Street in 1881. Isidor Lowenberg was granted a patent for an improvement to work pants in December 1879. His patented design used a widened, peculiarly shaped waistband to reinforce the front pocket corners, the small (watch) pocket corners, and one corner of the rear pocket. The back-straps were positioned to reinforce the other corner of the rear pocket (patent illustration). It is assumed that the firm of *Meyerstein & Lowenberg* began manufacturing work pants using this patented design in about 1880.

The partnership continued until 1887 when Isidor started a clothing wholesale business down the street at 20 Sansome–*Lowenberg & Company*–with his son Albert. Lewis Meyerstein continued in clothing manufacturing under his own name at 109 Sansome until his son joined him in the business in 1894. After Isidor left the company, Lewis, who remained at the same business address, may have continued to manufacture the patented pants until 1890 when riveting became generally available. An article in an 1889 issue of the Daily Alta California described the two firms as both manufacturing over-

Lewis Meyerstein

alls under the brand name of "Pacific Coast." These may have been the patent design. No examples of pants made using the *Meyerstein & Lowenberg* patented design were available for study at the time of writing.

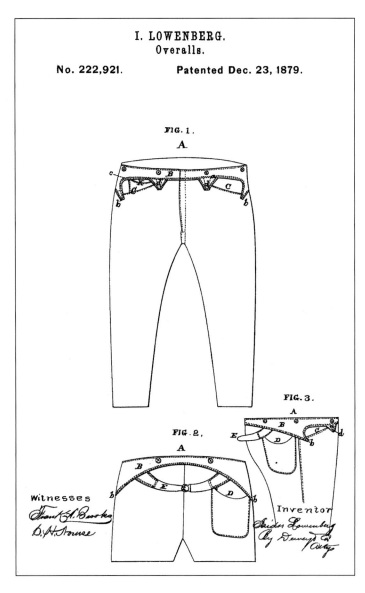

This patent is for an elaborate waistband cut to cover both front and one back pocket corner. I believe that I have seen a fragment of jeans made with this patent design, but I do not have a photograph of it.

In addition to the patented waistband shape, there is a lot of cross-stitching called for in the description.

UNITED STATES PATENT OFFICE.

ISIDOR LOWENBERG, OF SAN FRANCISCO, CALIFORNIA.

IMPROVEMENT IN OVERALLS.

Specification forming part of Letters Patent No. **222,921**, dated December 23, 1879; application filed June 10, 1879.

To all whom it may concern:

Be it known that I, ISIDOR LOWENBERG, of the city and county of San Francisco, and State of California, have invented an Improvement in Overalls; and I hereby declare the following to be a full, clear, and exact description thereof.

My invention relates to certain improvements in the manufacture of overalls, pants, and other similar garments; but it is especially adapted to overalls which are of coarse strong material, and adapted for outside wear.

It consists in the combination of a peculiarly-shaped waistband, either with or without re-enforcing projections for the pocket-openings, with a peculiarly-curved back-strap in two pieces, and cut independent of the waistband, the free ends of said strap being nearly or quite horizontal, while the opposite ends curve upward and backward beneath the waistband, as is more fully described in the accompanying drawings, in which—

Figure 1 is a front view. Fig. 2 is a rear view. Fig. 3 is a side view.

Let A represent the overalls or pants, and B the waistband, which I cut in a peculiar shape, so that it shall, while in one piece, perform more than one office in binding and strengthening the overalls. The overalls are provided with the usual front pockets, C, and rear pockets, D, which are duly strengthened by cross-stitching *a* at the corners, as shown.

The rear portion of the waistband is widened or extended down to a point at the hips, as shown at *b*, so as to cover the hip-seam and form a re-enforce to it. The extended portions also cover one corner of both rear and front pockets. This extension *b* is cross-stitched at its end, so as to still further strengthen it, the hip-seam, and corner of pocket. In fact it does away with any necessity of extra re-enforces at the pocket-corners.

The waistband passes along the upper corner, *c*, of the small pocket *k*, and may have extensions *d*, forming part of the waistband, to secure the inner corner, *a*, of the front pockets, as shown. These extensions are cut with the waistband and have double lines of stitching upon them, as shown.

The back-straps E are formed of two pieces cut with a peculiar curve, so that while the ends which are united by the buckle will be horizontal, the rear ends will curve upward and backward so as to pass beneath the waistband, where they are stitched, so that they not only assist in strengthening the back part of the overalls, where the strain of suspenders would fall, but they are doubly secured by the overlapping waistband.

Having thus described my invention, what I claim as new, and desire to secure by Letters Patent, is—

The waistband B, formed with the broad downwardly-projecting side pieces, *b*, and the pocket-re-enforcing strips *d*, in combination with the independent curved back-straps E, having their free ends meeting in a line, while their opposite ends pass upward and are stitched beneath the waistband, substantially as herein described.

In witness whereof I have hereunto set my hand.

ISIDOR LOWENBERG.

Witnesses:
GEO. H. STRONG,
FRANK A. BROOKS.

Felix Kivi was born in Prussia in about 1850. Felix moved with his wife and two children from New York to San Francisco in 1880. In 1881, he was listed in a San Francisco City Directory as a "cutter" for *A. B. Elfelt & Co.*, a clothing manufacturer. Cutters cut cloth from the bolts into pieces to be sewn together to make the clothes. Felix was granted a patent for an improvement to work pants in 1881. But, the patent was not for a design to strengthen pants, but for a double pocket and long draw strap as an extension of the cinch strap. However, the patent illustration shows a unique strengthening design for the front pockets. This same design is also shown on his second patent for an improvement to the fly of overalls and pants. It is guessed that Felix was never granted a patent for this pocket strengthening improvement.

In 1884, he went to work as a cutter for *I X L*, a large auction house dealing in clothing and men's furnishing goods (illustration). In 1887, he went into business for himself as a tailor at 1243 Folsom Street. He apparently never went into clothing manufacturing. If his unpatented design for strengthening pockets on overalls was used, it may have been by one of the companies he worked for (*A. B. Elfelt* or *I X L*). He was still an independent tailor living in San Francisco in 1910 and by 1930 he was retired.

There are no known examples of pants made using Felix Kivi's unpatented design for strengthening pockets. The illustration shows separate pieces of material sewn to the tops of the front pockets. One end of the pieces, nearest the fly, has tabs of material that are sewn under the waistband. The other end extends beyond the side seams to the back pocket; at the side seams they go to the inside of the pants. If a pair is found, it may also have one or more of his other three patented designs.

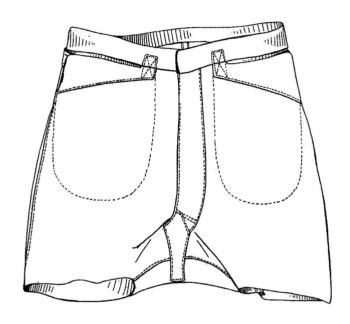

Inventor: Felix Kivi

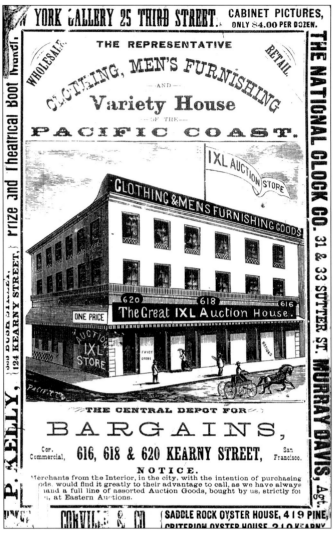

An advertisement for the IXL Auction House, from the cover of an 1875 San Francisco City directory.

(No Model.)

F. KIVI.
OVERALLS.

No. 249,187.   Patented Nov. 8, 1881.

Fig. 1.

A.

Fig. 2.

A.

Witnesses:
W. Voit
Wm F. Clark

Inventor:
Felix Kivi.
By his Attys.,
Boone & Osborn

This patent illustration and an illustration for another patent by Felix Kivi both include a drawing of a pair of pants with the same pocket strengthening design that is not part of either patent claim. I presume that the design was not granted a patent, perhaps because of its similarity to an earlier patent such as Samuel Krouses' 1880 patent.

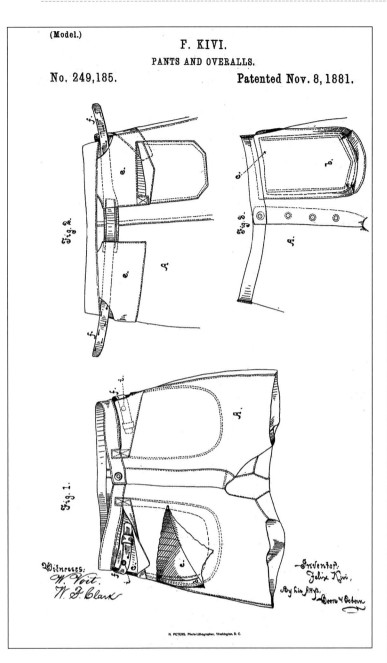

The other patent by Felix Kivi with an illustration for a pocket strengthening design that was not granted a patent. A similar instance was the patent of J. Wahl of Chicago, Illinois, that is described in a later chapter.

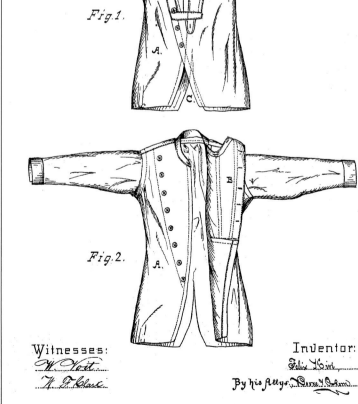

Felix Kivi was granted three patents on the same day. This is the third one. Nice looking shirt.

Banner Brothers

Banner Brothers first appears in San Francisco directories in 1873. Peter and Samuel Banner were the principals. The company imported and manufactured clothing and gents' furnishing goods at 104 and 106 Sansome Street. Peter Banner resided at 40 Geary Street in San Francisco and his brother Samuel lived in New York. In 1877, the business moved to the northeast corner of Sutter and Sansome streets. Pincus Banner is first listed as living in San Francisco in 1881, taking Peter's place as a principal in the company. However, Pincus Banner's patent was granted in 1879 in San Francisco. So, he may have arrived earlier without being listed in the directory.

I have not seen a pair of pants with this particular patent design. If one is found, it will likely have a "BB" monogram on it, as Banner Brothers registered this trademark in 1878.

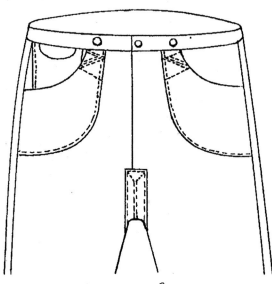

Inventor
Pincus Banner

Sansome street, corner of Market. 1883?

The date of 1883, written below the photograph, is probably correct. Banner Brothers were at this location from 1878 to 1886. (The "GUNS" sign on the roof is not part of the Banner Brothers' sign.)

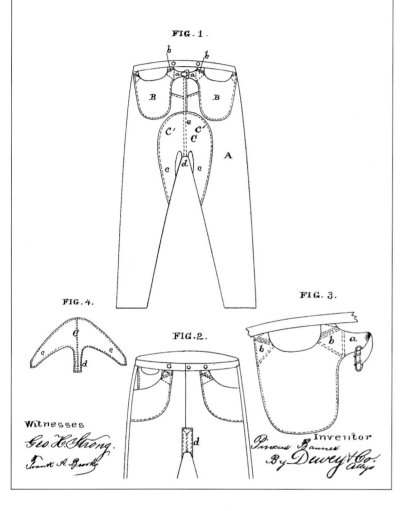

P. BANNER.
Overalls.

No. 218,472.　　　Patented Aug. 12, 1879.

FIG. 1.

FIG. 4.　　　　　　　　　　FIG. 3.

FIG. 2.

Witnesses
Geo. H. Strong.
Frank A. Brooks.

Inventor
Pincus Banner
By Dewey & Co.
Attys.

A Banner Brothers ad in the wholesale clothing section of Langley's 1876 San Francisco City Directory.

This patent is for an interesting crotch and seat strengthening design, but does not include the pocket strengthening design shown.

UNITED STATES PATENT OFFICE

PINCUS BANNER, OF SAN FRANCISCO, CALIFORNIA.

IMPROVEMENT IN OVERALLS.

Specification forming part of Letters Patent No. **218,472**, dated August 12, 1879; application filed May 14, 1879.

To all whom it may concern:

Be it known that I, PINCUS BANNER, of the city and county of San Francisco, and State of California, have invented an Improvement in Overalls; and I hereby declare the following to be a full, clear, and exact description thereof.

My invention relates to certain improvements in wearing apparel, and is more especially adapted to overalls for outside wear and pants which are made of heavy material, for miners and those engaged in rough heavy work.

My invention consists in a peculiar re-enforce for the seat, which is formed with three extensions or projections, two of which extend down the inside leg-seams, while the third extends over the middle seam up to the front opening of the pants. The corners of the pocket-openings are prevented from being torn out by a peculiar system of cross-stitching, so that I am enabled to dispense with all supplemental re-enforcing-pieces at these points.

Referring to the accompanying drawings for a more complete explanation of my invention, Figure 1 is a rear view of my overalls. Fig. 2 is a front view. Fig. 3 is an enlarged view of the pocket. Fig. 4 is the rear re-enforce.

Let A represent the seat or rear portion of a pair of overalls, and B the rear pockets, one of which is placed on each hip. Each of these pockets is cut out in one piece, in such a shape that the upper inner corner, *a*, forms half of the back strap, as shown. When stitched in place the pockets are cross-stitched at the corners, as shown at *b*, so as to strengthen them at those points, and the stitching not only serves to secure the pockets firmly, but the outer end of the parts of the straps *b*, forming part of the pockets. The pockets and straps therefore form a continuous re-enforce when the two ends of the straps are buckled together. Any strain on the upper portion of the pants is met by the peculiar formation of the pockets and straps, where the cloth is doubled, and where the stitching is provided to resist strains.

The re-enforce C is formed with the seat portions C' C' and three extensions or projections, two of which form leg-seam re-enforces *c*, and the other an extension or tongue, *d*, which is sewed onto both sides of the center-seam, passing down under the crotch or middle seam up to the lower part of the front opening of the pants, as shown.

I am aware that re-enforces have previously been made for the seat of pants; but mine is made in such a peculiar shape that it not only forms double cloths for that portion most subject to friction and wear, but also strengthens the leg and crotch seams, which are more liable to rip or tear apart than any other in the pants. The seat re-enforce is not only sewed around the edges with double stitches, but a center seam, *c*, of double stitching is made, which starts from the upper end of the re-enforce C, and is continued down the center-band *d* for its whole length, thus giving additional strength.

By cutting the pocket pieces and straps in one piece and the seat re-enforce with its extensions in one piece, and also providing cross-stitching at the corners of the pockets, I am enabled to do away with all necessity of supplemental separate re-enforce pieces for either pockets or center-seams, thus simplifying and cheapening the construction of the overalls.

Having thus described my invention, what I claim as new, and desire to secure by Letters Patent, is—

In a pair of pantaloons or overalls, the re-enforce C, consisting of the seat portions C' C', extensions *c c*, and tongue *d*, formed and attached to the pantaloons, substantially as described, and for the purpose of strengthening the leg and crotch seams of the garment, as specified.

In witness whereof I have hereunto set my hand.

PINCUS BANNER.

Witnesses:
DAVID EISNER,
EMIL GUNZBURGER.

Although the "peculiar system of cross-stitching" is described in the patent and shown as strengthening the pockets in the illustration, it is not claimed as part of the patent. I have not seen a pair of pants made by Banner Brothers, so I don't know if the "peculiar system of cross-stitching" was used in production. This patent is an indication that stitching variations were not patentable, like the triangular stitch pattern on the Neustadter Brothers "Boss of the Road" brand.

Yung Chow

Yung Chow was granted two patents in 1878 for designs that would strengthen work pants. Yung Chow was living in San Francisco at the time of his patent applications. There is a listing in the 1870 U.S. Census record that could be him (the hand written records often are difficult to read). If it is, he was thirty-two years old at the time and was a merchant. It is unfortunate that the record is so lacking, as it would be interesting to know more about the challenges faced by an Asian competing in a market that was largely dominated by Eastern Europeans. Clearly, Mr. Chow was a talented, innovative thinker whose designs were both beautiful and functional.

It is not known if either of his patented designs was ever used in manufacturing work pants. His two patents were for strengthening pockets. The first design had the inner pocket formed from a single piece of material with its seam at the center of the pocket opening instead of a corner (patent illustration). The second patent strengthened the pocket by enclosing a cord or welt of twisted material in the edge of the pocket (patent illustration). There are some examples of pants that were constructed somewhat like Chow's second patent; however, the similarities are not sufficient to justify any assumptions.

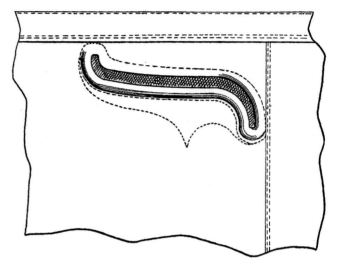

Inventor

Yung Chow

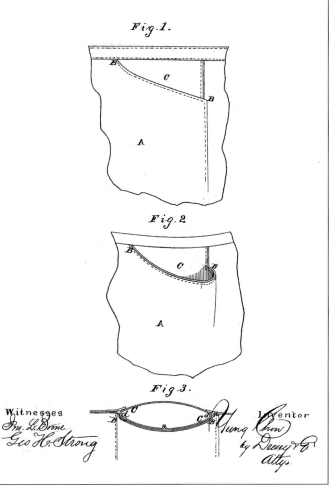

Y. CHOW.
Pocket.

No. 201,595.   Patented March 26, 1878.

Fig.1.

Fig.2

Fig.3.

Witnesses   Inventor

This patent uses one piece of material, ringing the inside of the pocket, to strengthen the corners. Pants using this patent design would be difficult to recognize because of the lack of any notable pattern.

UNITED STATES PATENT OFFICE.

YUNG CHOW, OF SAN FRANCISCO, CALIFORNIA.

IMPROVEMENT IN POCKETS.

Specification forming part of Letters Patent No. **201,595**, dated March 26, 1878; application filed January 14, 1878.

To all whom it may concern:

Be it known that I, YUNG CHOW, of the city and county of San Francisco, State of California, have invented an Improved Pocket for Clothing; and I do hereby declare the following description and accompanying drawings are sufficient to enable any person skilled in the art or science to which it most nearly appertains to make and use my said invention without further invention or experiment.

My invention relates to certain improvements in the manufacture of clothing; and it consists in a novel method of constructing the pockets so that the pocket itself forms a re-enforce to prevent the breaking or tearing out of the corners of the pocket-opening, which is made in the material to receive the pocket.

Referring to the accompanying drawings, Figures 1 and 2 are views of my invention. Fig. 3 is a section of the same.

A is a portion of a pair of overalls, pants, or other article of clothing, and B shows a pocket-opening formed in the usual manner.

As these pocket-openings are subjected to severe strains at the corners, various methods for re-enforcing or strengthening them have been resorted to, such as rivets, strips of material, either formed in cutting out the goods or independently, and sewed across the corner seams of the pocket, and also by making the opening itself with rounded corners.

In my invention I do away with the neces-sity of these devices, by so constructing the pocket C that there are no corner-seams, and the cloth is continuous at the point where the corners of the pocket-opening are formed, so as to re-enforce these points without the necessity of extra pieces of any sort.

The pocket C has its front edge stitched to the edge of the pocket-opening B, as shown, and it continues in a curve, d, extending upward across and past the corners of the opening.

The pocket itself is made of one piece of material, and so folded that the seam falls in the middle of one side, thus avoiding all seams at the corners and sides.

Having thus described my invention, what I claim as new, and desire to secure by Letters Patent, is—

The pocket C, stitched to the edges of the pocket-opening B, and arranged to have its seam intermediate of the sides, leaving the fabric of the pocket continuous and without seam at the sides and corners, and extending up over the corners, so as to form a re-enforce, substantially as described.

In witness whereof I have hereunto set my hand.

YUNG CHOW.

Witnesses:
GEO. H. STRONG,
FRANK A. BROOKS.

Notice in the fifth paragraph the mention of earlier patents using rivets (Jacob Davis) and pockets with rounded openings (Antonio Pena).

125

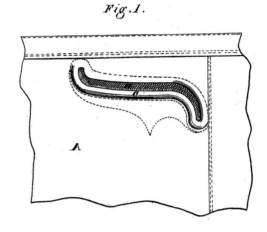

Y. CHOW.
Pocket for Garments.

No. 204,199.   Patented May 28, 1878.

Fig.1.

A

Fig.2.

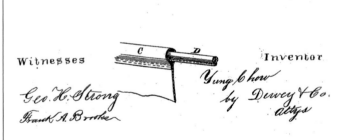

Witnesses   Inventor
Geo. H. Strong   Yung Chow
Frank A. Brooks   by Dewey & Co.
                                                        attys

The illustration for this patent shows a pocket opening with a peculiar shape. I have not seen any like it; although, I have seen piping around the openings of some pants pockets.

In Chow's earlier patent, he merely referred to Jacob Davis's use of rivets in his patent. In this patent Chow asserted, "I do away with unsightly rivets."

UNITED STATES PATENT OFFICE.

YUNG CHOW, OF SAN FRANCISCO, CALIFORNIA.

IMPROVEMENT IN POCKETS FOR GARMENTS.

Specification forming part of Letters Patent No. **204,199**, dated May 28, 1878; application filed April 10, 1878.

To all whom it may concern:

Be it known that I, YUNG CHOW, of the city and county of San Francisco, and State of California, have invented an Improved Pocket for Garments; and I do hereby declare the following to be a full, clear, and exact description thereof, reference being had to the accompanying drawings.

My invention relates to certain improvements in the construction of pockets for garments, by which I am enabled to strengthen them, and prevent them from being torn out at the corners or sides by the strains to which they are exposed; and it consists in the employment of a strip of leather, cloth, or other suitable material, which is rolled or twisted into a stout welt or cord, and is inclosed in a shirr or elongated opening, which extends partly or entirely around the pocket-opening, thus resisting strain at the corners and other points.

This device is especially adapted to be used upon heavy duck goods, overalls, and such clothing as is used in mining, lumbering, harvesting, and all sorts of heavy work, and it will be more completely explained by referring to the accompanying drawings, in which—

Figure 1 is a view of the pocket-opening with my attachment complete. Fig. 2 is a view of the cord or strengthening-strip.

A is the body of the article of clothing, and B is the pocket-opening. This opening may be made of any desired shape, this not being material to the success of my invention. I can, therefore, make an angular or curved pocket, or one with rounded corners, at pleasure, to suit the position or requirements of the pocket. Around the corners or the whole pocket-opening I form an elongated shirr or tube of the material, by stitching down or folding over the material, as shown at C. I also make a stout cord, D, of leather or other material, which may be rolled or twisted into shape to fit into this tube surrounding the pocket. I prefer, however, to make this welt by folding or rolling up a strip of the material and stitching it, as this material will not shrink when the goods are washed, and it is very strong. This strip is laid into the tube and stitched in by surrounding it by the material when the tube is formed; or, if desired, it might be stitched through, although I do not think this especially necessary or desirable. By this construction I am enabled to greatly strengthen the pocket-opening, so that it will be impossible to tear it out; and I do away with unsightly rivets, strengthening cross-pieces at the corners, &c.

Having thus described my invention, I do not claim, broadly, the use of a cording, as I am aware that this is used upon the edges of dresses, and in other places for ornamental effect; but I am not aware that a pocket-opening has ever been strengthened or re-enforced by any such device as I have shown.

What I claim as new, therefore, and desire to secure by Letters Patent, is—

The improvement in the method of re-enforcing the mouths or openings of pockets for garments, consisting in partly or wholly surrounding such openings with a strip or welt of strengthening material, D, inclosed in a tube formed by the stitching C, and applied substantially as shown and described.

In witness whereof I hereunto set my hand and seal.

YUNG CHOW. [L. S.]

Witnesses:
GEO. H. STRONG,
FRANK A. BROOKS.

Although these denim pants do not use any piping around the pockets, they do have the design stitch that is illustrated on the patent, suggesting that these might be examples of Yung Chow's work.

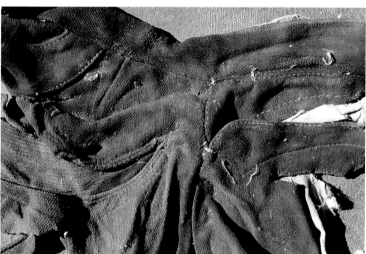

An example of wool pants with the same design stitch on the front pockets.

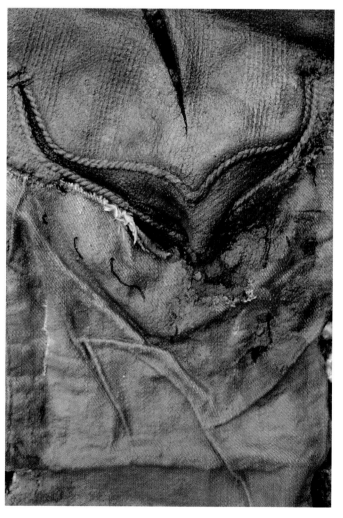

This example of the back pocket of a pair of woolen pants illustrates the use of piping (or in this case rope) to re-enforce the edge of the pocket, which was mentioned in the Chow patents. However, his patent describes the piping as being enclosed in a tube, so his patent may not cover this.

127

Charles A. Jones

Charles Augustus Jones was granted a patent for improved work pants in December 1879. The patent design was for a double layer of material on the outside of the entire upper part of the pants. Since he went into business in 1880 as an importer of dry goods and gents' furnishing goods, he may have manufactured and sold them himself. His business address at 113 Sansome Street was in the heart of the commercial clothing-manufacturing district. But he lasted just one year. One example of these pants has a partially readable cloth label that reads "UNION PACIFIC." It may be that these pants were specifically marketed to railroad workers.

Another possibility is that Charles Jones sold his patent rights to *Heynemann & Co.* There is a pair of work pants of the *Heynemann & Co.'s* noted "Can't Bust 'Em" brand made after 1900 that uses the main design elements of Jones's patent. These pants are pictured in the chapter on Post-1890 Work Pants.

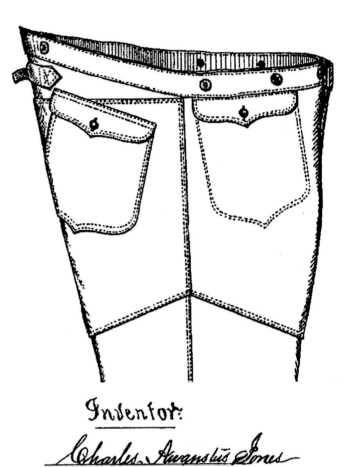

Inventor:

Charles Augustus Jones

Front of a pair of denim jeans made using Jones's patent design. To my knowledge, this the first instance of pocket flaps used on work pants. The white spots are candle wax drippings. (courtesy of Hitoshi Yamada)

Back of the same jeans: The seam
for the second layer of material on
the upper part can be clearly seen.
(courtesy of Hitoshi Yamada)

Upper front part of the Jones patent jeans. (courtesy of Hito-shi Yamada)

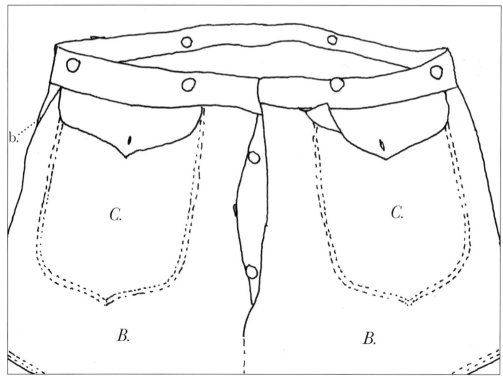

Upper front part of the Jones patent jeans. (courtesy of Hitoshi Yamada)

131

The left front pocket flap raised to show the watch pocket construction—much like the Neustadter Brothers "Boss of the Road" pants with the Gibbons patent-like extended, vertical corner seams. (courtesy of Hitoshi Yamada)

The upper back of the Jones jeans. (courtesy of Hitoshi Yamada)

A : overalls
B.' : separate piece covering top part of overalls
C. : pocket
b'. : princple seams that attach separate piece

Close-up of the left front pocket top showing stitching details. (courtesy of Hitoshi Yamada)

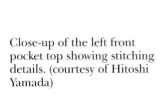

Close-up of the leather label on the Jones patent pants. The words "UNION PACIFIC" can be read. There is also a barely legible date— 1879—the date of the Jones patent. (courtesy of Hitoshi Yamada)

This patent uses a second layer of material over the entire upper part of the pants, and reinforces the pocket openings by having them be formed of both layers. The pockets are made by sewing both layers together in the shapes of pockets.

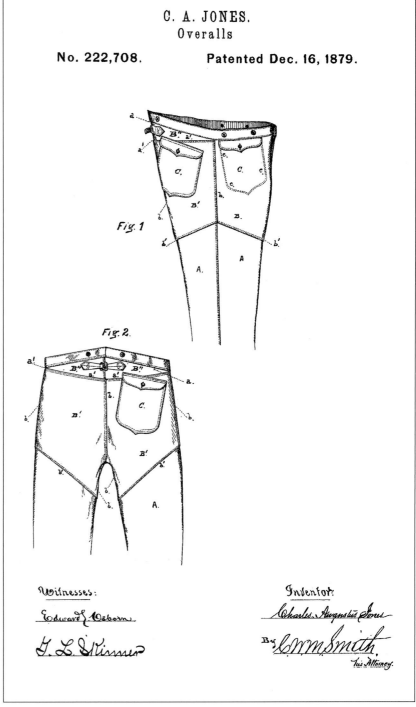

C. A. JONES.
Overalls

No. 222,708.   Patented Dec. 16, 1879.

Fig. 1

Fig. 2

Witnesses:
Edward J. Osborn.
G. L. Skinner.

Inventor:
Charles Augustus Jones
By C. W. M. Smith.
his Attorney.

133

Pre-1873 Work Pants

Work pants sold in the American West before 1873 were manufactured mostly on the East Coast, with New York being the prime production center. There was little or no development aimed at strengthening these early pants. Patented innovations were designed predominantly for non-work pants. Patents were granted for such things as prevention of pick-pocketing (Fenner Darling, 1861), convenience of voiding oneself (Ehlers Herron, 1862), devices for holding the cuffs down (Samuel Heller, 1863), simplicity of manufacturing (Harmon Osler, 1863), making the waist adjustable (B. J. Greely, 1965), and adding stretching to the knees (T.

R. Sloan, 1870). The illustrations for these patents are shown at the end of this chapter.

The waist overalls of that era were simple and utilitarian, with scant effort in design to reduce wear damage. Something else of mention is that I have yet to see a pair of workpants dateable to before 1873 with either a watch pocket or a back pocket. It is possible that Jacob Davis was the first to add these features to work pants he began making in Reno in 1871 and 1872.

The pictured examples that are in this chapter are typical of the pre-1873 work pants that I have seen in photographs or that I have had in my hands.

Looking down Market Street in 1868. Work pants were being shipped to San Francisco from the East Coast on the many Clipper ships that can be seen docked in the Bay.

A pair of pre-1873 denim waist pants. I have heard that a nearly identical pair of pants was marked as Army issue. These are unmarked. I think that they are Civil War-era pants.

Back of the Civil War-era(?) pants.

Top front of Civil War-era(?) pants. Like most pre-1873 work pants, these have no watch pocket, upwardly convex front pocket tops, and are made of lightweight denim.

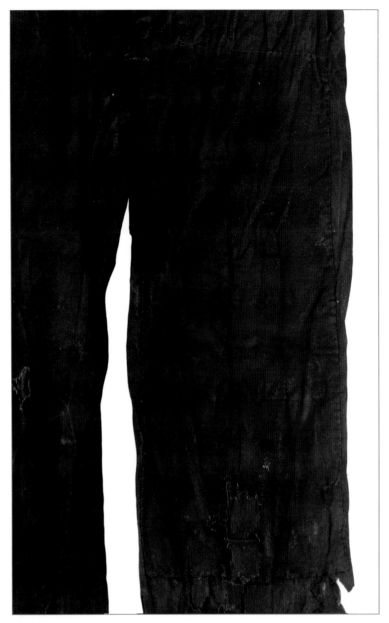

Close-up of upper right leg of the Civil War-era(?) pants showing the extensive patching on the crotch and leg.

Close-up of the cinch strap on the Civil war-era(?) pants, showing that it is positioned high—partly on the waistband—and that the attachment is small and weak.

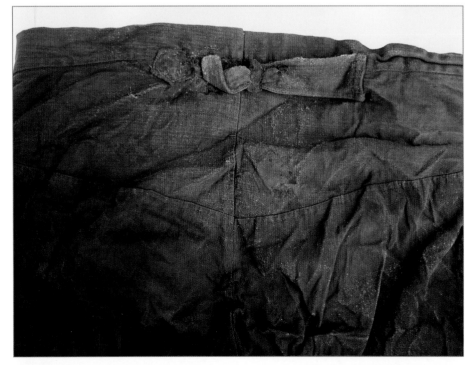

Upper back of the Civil War-era(?) pants.

Inside top of the Civil War-era(?) pants, showing the front pocket bag made of thin cotton.

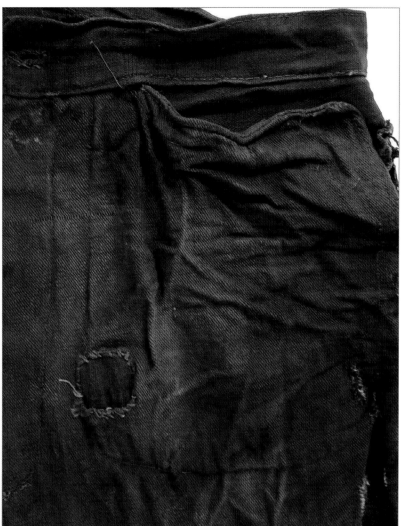

Right front pocket area of a pair of pre-1873 waist overall denim work pants showing the typical 'sailor' cut of the pocket top. The denim is light weight.

There was extensive patching done to the fly of these Civil War-era(?) pants.

The right half of the pair of pre-1873 work pants made of lightweight denim. This style of work pants had nothing extra done to strengthen their weak points.

Back of the pre-1873 denim work pants showing the typical small cinch strap and split back.

The top back of a pair of work pants that may be tailor-made. They are made in a pre-1873 style—lightweight denim, no back pocket, small cinch strap, and a split back. Note that at the bottom seam of the yoke is on the outside—a construction not typical of production-wear.

Left front of the tailor-made(?) denim pants. Typical of pre-1873-style work pants are the cut of the pocket top and the lack of a watch pocket. Note that the stitching on these pants is very uneven—more so than the worst that I've seen on production pants.

Close-up of the front pocket of a pre-1873 denim waist overall work pants. Pants like these could be cheaply produced on the East Coast and shipped to San Francisco by the thousands.

Close-up of the cinch strap crossing the split back on the pre-1873 denim work pants. Note the large yoke.

The left side of the pre-1873 denim work pants. They have a sewn-on front pocket, a small cinch strap, no back pocket and no watch pocket, are made of lightweight denim, and have a split back. The waistband is very narrow on this pair.

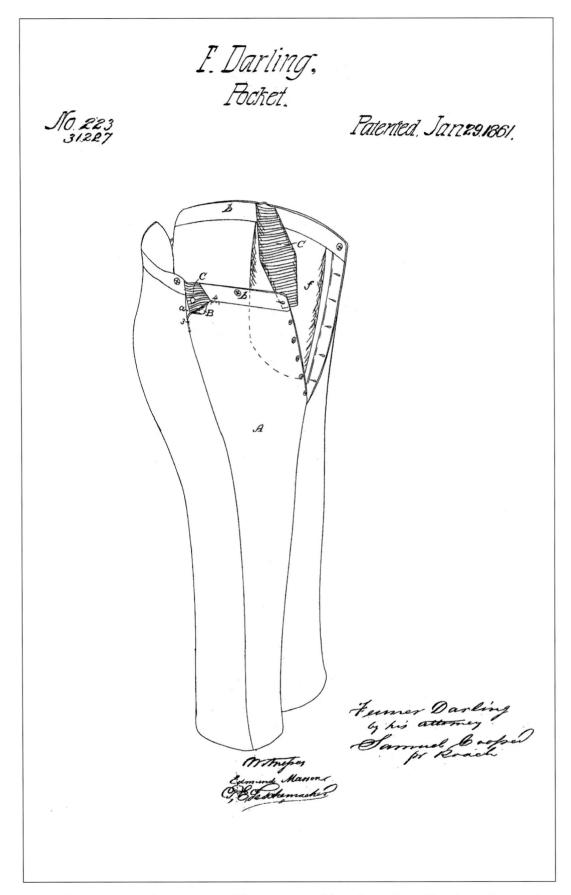

F. Darling,
Pocket.

No. 223
31,227

Patented. Jan.29.1861.

This earlier 1861 patent for pants was an idea to prevent pick-pocketing by making the pocket opening so small that a hand could not be easily inserted. (The pants wearer might have the same difficulty.)

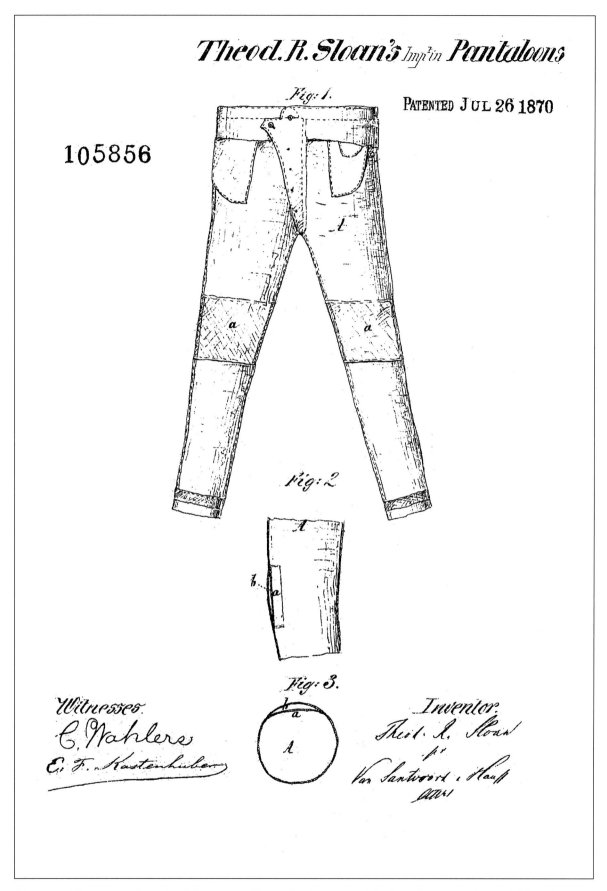

A knee-padding patent from 1870. The pants illustration is very crudely done. I suppose the model for this patent may have been made as crudely.

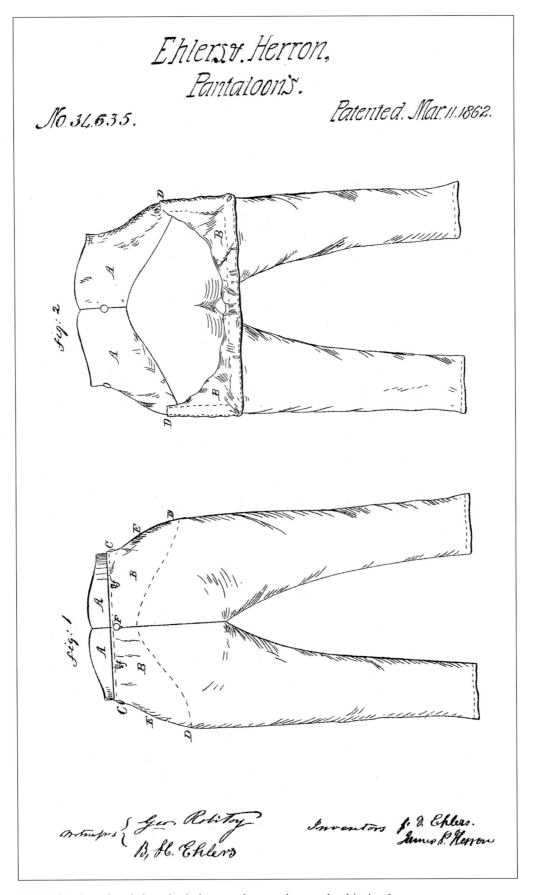

Ehlers & Herron,
Pantaloons.

No. 34,635.

Patented. Mar. 11. 1862.

Fig. 2

Fig. 1

Witnesses { Geo. Robitoy
B. H. Ehlers

Inventors J. D. Ehlers.
James P. Herron

OK. Didn't they already have back doors on long underwear by this time?

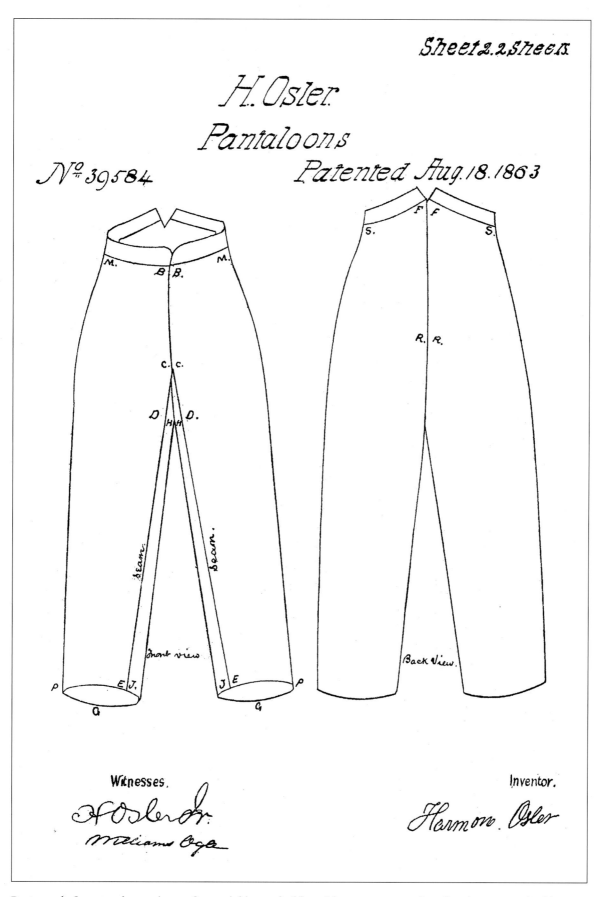

Sheet 2. 2 Sheets

H. Osler
Pantaloons

No. 39584

Patented Aug. 18. 1863

Front view

Back View

Witnesses.

Inventor.

Harmon. Osler

Pants made from two large pieces of material instead of four. I have seen examples of work pants made this way. They often have a fake seam on the outside of the leg.

S. Heller.
Pantaloon Strap.
№ 40931.
Patented Dec. 15. 1863.
Fig. 1.

Fig. 2.

Witnesses.

Inventor.
Samuel Heller.

A gentleman's pant legs wouldn't ride up while using this patent devise.

B. J. GREELY.
PANTALOONS.

No. 50,242.

Patented Oct. 3, 1865.

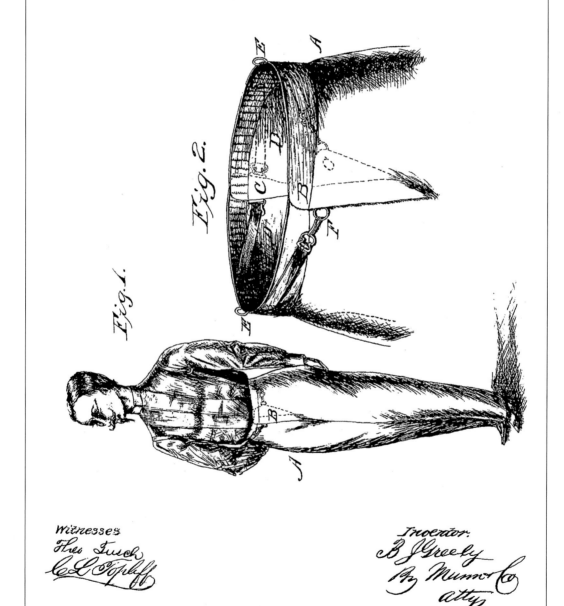

An easily opened and closed fly.

Post-1890 Work Pants

Work pants dateable to after 1890 are nearly all made with rivet reinforcement. Jacob Davis's patent ran out in 1890 and riveting became available to every company. I have only seen one of the non-riveted patent designs, described in the earlier chapters that were manufactured after 1890—a pair of "Can't Bust 'Em" brand work pants made after 1900 that were made using the Charles A. Jones patent design. It would probably require detailed records of the early 1890s from the companies to find if any of the other non-riveted patent designs were continued. However, the fires following the 1906 earthquake destroyed all of the records of the San Francisco companies.

A pair of duck "Can't Bust 'Em" overalls. This was a brand name for Heynemann & Co. trade-marked in 1879. They are made with a double layer of material above the knees. This was a design patented by Charles A. Jones in 1879—the same year. But, these pants were made much later; certainly after 1900, and probably as late as the 1930s. They have belt loops and no cinch strap, but there are suspender buttons. (courtesy of Mike Hodis)

Back of the duck "Can't Bust 'Em" overalls. The double layering was not extended into the crotch area. (courtesy of Mike Hodis)

Close-up of the "Can't Bust 'Em" label on the duck overalls. No maker is given but it is likely the Eloesser-Heynemann Co. (courtesy of Mike Hodis)

148

A pair of twentieth century Lee Jeans. Pictured are close-ups of the right front pocket, the label, an embossed button, and an unembossed button (courtesy of Mike Hodis)

Continued on following page

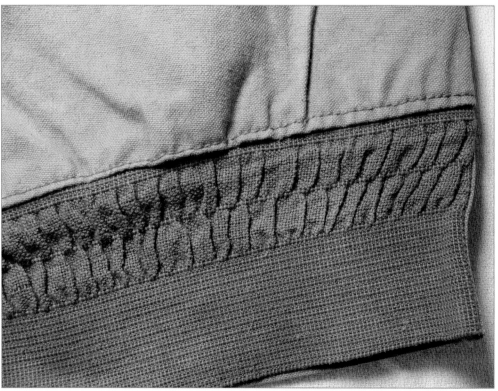

American Field Gun Coats duck pants made by the Hettrick Manufacturing Company of Toledo, Ohio. The suspender buttons are embossed: "LEVI STRAUSS & CO S.F.CAL" Pictured are close-ups of the leg cuff, both tags—one cloth, the other paper—an embossed suspender button front and back. (courtesy of Mike Hodis)

Continued on following page

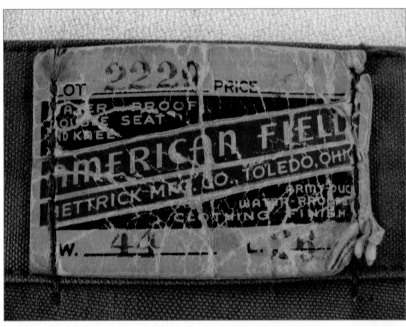

A pair of boy's denim waist overalls made, probably, in the 1890s. The fact that they are riveted places them after 1890, and the lack of belt loops and a second back pocket suggests that they are pre-1900. I think that these may have been made by Neustadter Brothers in San Francisco; the style of the suspender buttons and the design of the crotch reinforcement are similar to their "Boss of the Road" brand from that era. (courtesy of Hitoshi Yamada)

Upper front of the 1890s boy's pants. (courtesy of Hitoshi Yamada)

Upper back of the 1890s boy's pants. One back pocket and cinch strap without belt loops marks it as likely pre-1900. There were extra pieces of fabric sewn into the upper side seams, perhaps to accommodate a boy's growth. (courtesy of Hitoshi Yamada)

Close-up of the label on the 1890s boy's pants. The printing is almost, but not quite, readable. (courtesy of Hitoshi Yamada)

Close-up of the extra piece of material reinforcing the crotch of the 1890s boy's pants. It compares closely with that of the "Boss of the Road" pants construction from that period. (courtesy of Hitoshi Yamada)

A pair of brown duck waist overalls from, probably, the 1890s. The rivets mark them as post-1890 and the lack of belt loops and a second back pocket suggests that they were made before 1900. (courtesy of Hitoshi Yamada)

Upper front of the 1890s brown duck overalls. (courtesy of Hitoshi Yamada)

Upper back of the 1890s brown duck overalls. The back pocket has an arcuate-like stitch pattern on it. The cinch strap has the design of a non-riveted style, with the ends tucked up under the waistband. (courtesy of Hitoshi Yamada)

Close-up of the cloth label on the 1890s brown duck overalls. The maker might be identified either by the brand name "Eureka" or the monogram in the upper left corner. "Eureka" is the California State Motto. (courtesy of Hito-shi Yamada)

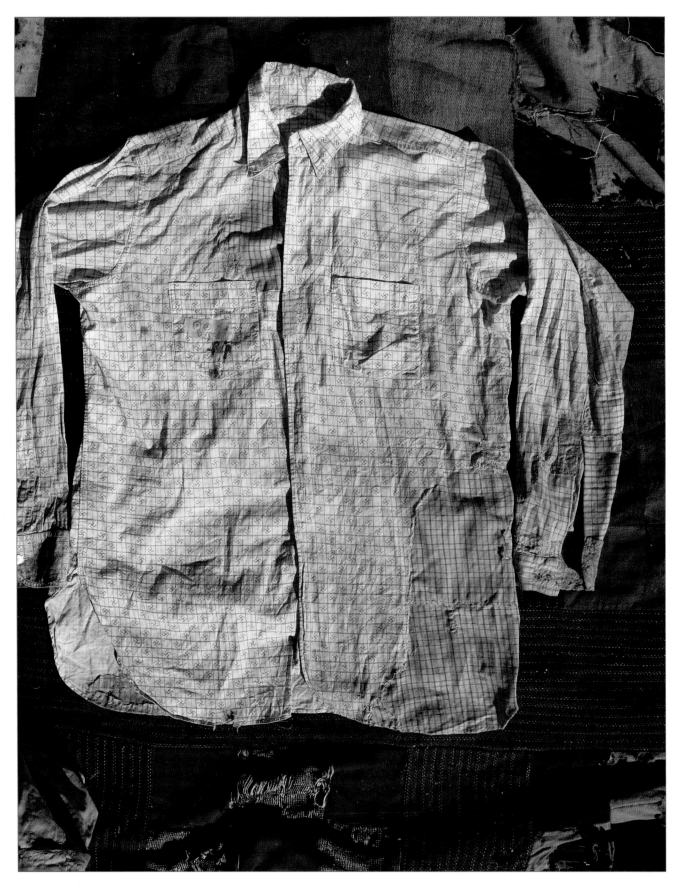

A later shirt made by Neustadter Brothers. Probably early twentieth century. (courtesy of Brit Eaton)

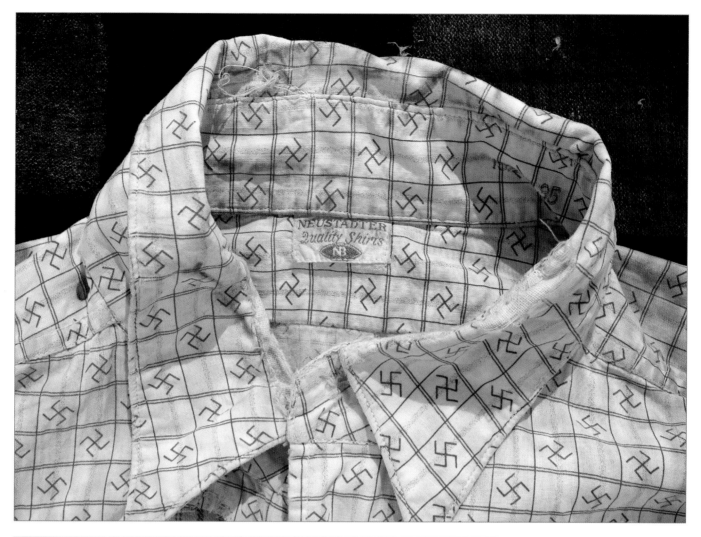

Close-up of the label on the early twentieth century Neustadter Brothers shirt. Note the design pattern--obviously pre-Nazi Germany. (courtesy of Brit Eaton)

A pair of "The Stronghold" jeans
ca. early 1900s. "The Stronghold"
was a Los Angeles California brand
that started in 1895. (courtesy of Brit
Eaton)

Top front of The Stronghold
jeans. Made after the Levi
Strauss & Co. rivet patent
expired in 1890. Other jean
manufacturers then were free
to copy the Levi Strauss & Co.
work pants. But, there are differences in this pair. The watch
pocket is not riveted and the
front pocket upper corner rivets
are on the waistband. (courtesy
of Brit Eaton)

Back of the early 1900s, The Stronghold jeans cinch strap is not riveted. The placement of the right-hand rivet on the back pockets looks shoddy. Note also that there are no design stitches on the back pockets. (courtesy of Brit Eaton)

Close-up of the cloth label on "The Stronghold" jeans. It is barely legible, but it says Los Angeles, Cal along the bottom edge. (courtesy of Brit Eaton)

A pair of Lee brand children's jeans from about the 1920s or 1930s. Note the arcuate design stitches on the back pockets. This was before Levi Strauss & Co. trademarked the stitch. (courtesy of Brit Eaton)

An adult-size pair of Lee brand jeans from the 1920s or 1930s. Again, the arcuate design stitches are on the back pockets. The adult pants include the cinch strap riveted—the child's jeans did not. (courtesy of Brit Eaton)

A pair of Levi Strauss & Co. jeans from after 1922 (the year belt loops where put on) and before 1936 when a red tab was added to the back right pocket edge. (courtesy of Brit Eaton)

Back of the 1922-1936 Levi Strauss & Co. jeans. They look basically the same as the late 1800s Levi Strauss & Co. jeans except for the second back pocket and the belt loops. (courtesy of Brit Eaton)

A pair of "Boss of the Road" jeans ca. 1890s(?). There are no belt loops. But they are riveted. The suspenders are still attached. (courtesy of Brit Eaton)

Label on the ca. 1890s(?) "Boss of the Road" jeans. These were made by Neustadter Brothers, probably in New York. (courtesy of Brit Eaton)

Back of the ca. 1890s(?) "Boss of the Road" jeans. Two back pockets, but an unriveted cinch strap. (courtesy of Brit Eaton)

163

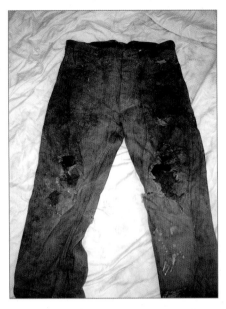

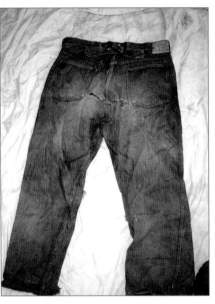

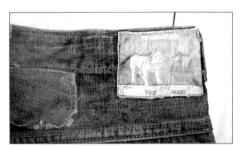

Label of the "Boss of the Road" jeans by Neustadter's. (courtesy of Brit Eaton)

"Boss of the Road" jeans by Neustadter Brothers. The belt loops date it as after 1900. (courtesy of Brit Eaton)

Back of the post-1900 "Boss of the Road" jeans. (courtesy of Brit Eaton)

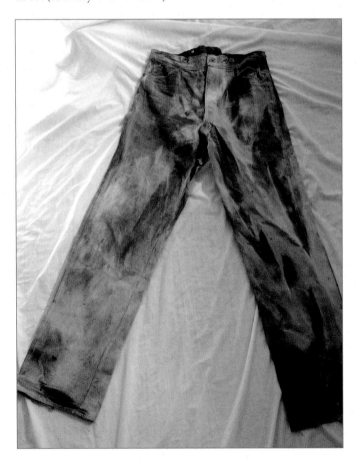

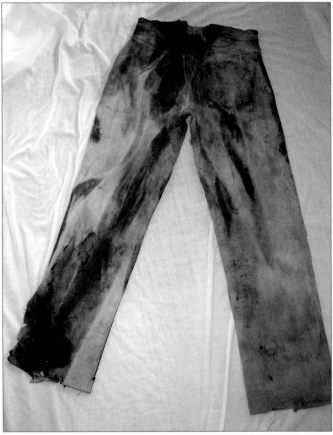

Pair of jeans from the 1890s. No belt loops, but it is riveted. The sun bleaching is extensive. (courtesy of Brit Eaton)

Back of 1890s jeans. (courtesy of Brit Eaton)

Top front of the 1890s jeans. The cut of the watch pocket is distinctive and there is a decorative stitch pattern on the pockets. (courtesy of Brit Eaton)

Top back of the 1890s jeans. The label is unreadable, and there is nothing distinctive about this pair of pants that would identify a maker. (courtesy of Brit Eaton)

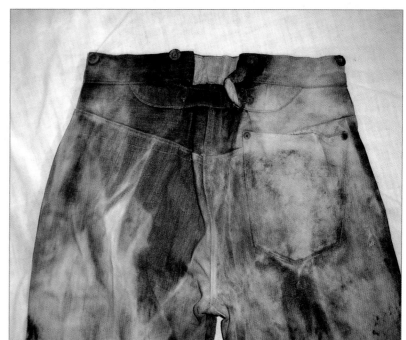

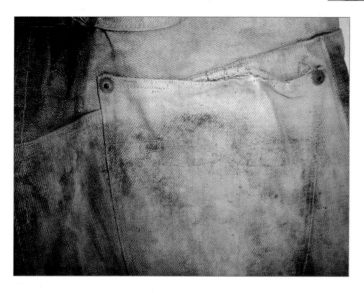

Back pocket of the 1890s jeans. Note the floral stitch pattern. I have seen this pattern on several brands of jeans from the late 1800s. (courtesy of Brit Eaton)

165

Additional Nineteenth Century Clothing Items from the Old West

In old photographs taken in mines, mining towns, and mills during the 1870s and 1880s, it can be seen that the clothing, other than work pants, was different than our's today and changed from decade to decade. I can almost tell the age of an old photograph of miners by the type of clothes they were wearing. In the 1870s, many of them wore pleated-front shirts and those who wore hats had on narrow-brimmed floppy ones. By the 1890s, the shirts were pleatless and the hats had wider and stiffer brims.

The following images are of items that came from the West, including women's and children's clothes. I am including them in this book because they create more of a picture of who the inhabitants of the West were and how they lived their lives. On the little boy's blue and white shirt you can clearly see his suspender marks crisscrossing the back and coming down the front of the shirt. Slightly burnt iron marks, and the outline of the iron used can be seen on several of the garments. Patching was widely practiced, showing how valuable the garments were to the people who wore them. The tags and patches have a wider date range than the other items; some are even vintage rather than antique.

What cannot be seen in old black-and-white photographs are the colors of the fabric pattern. I have included a montage of some of the fabric patterns I have seen that date from the 1870s and 1880s.

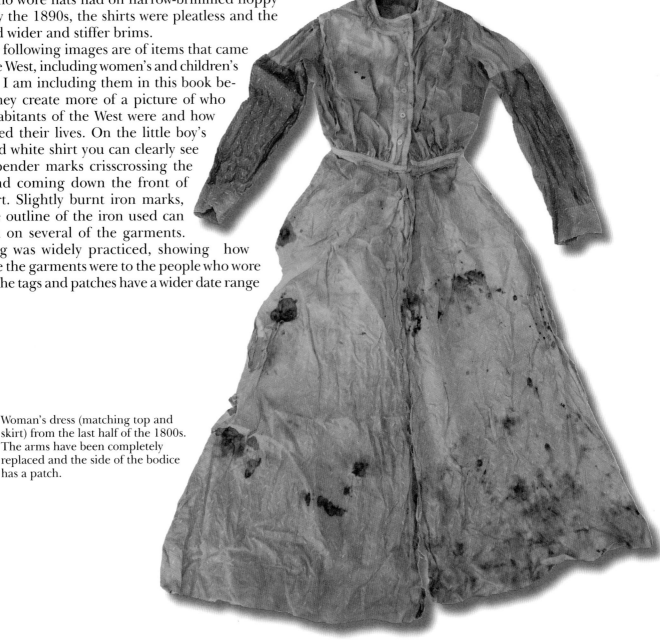

Woman's dress (matching top and skirt) from the last half of the 1800s. The arms have been completely replaced and the side of the bodice has a patch.

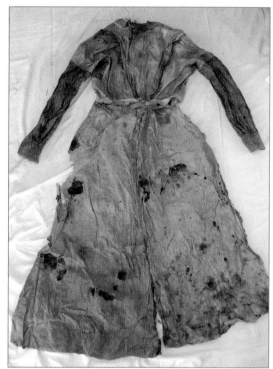

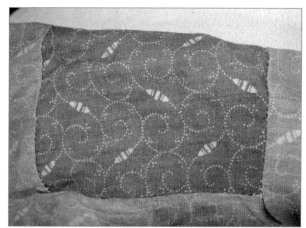

Close-up of the patchwork on the side of the bodice. The woman who owned this dress lived in a remote mining town in the 1870s and went to great length to keep it mended.

Close-up of the lacework on the bodice of the dress.

Back of the late 1800s woman's dress.

Boy's shirt from the late 1800s.

Back of the boy's shirt. Notice the "V" of less sun-faded material where the boy's suspenders were.

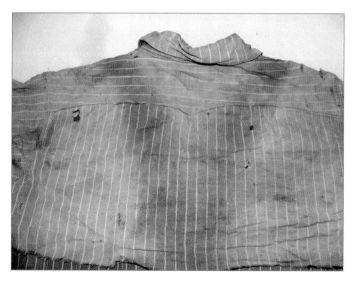

Close-ups of the arms showing the extensive patchwork. The boy lived in a remote mining town in the 1870s and was likely the child of the woman who owned the dress in the previous pictures. All of their clothes were kept patched and usable as long as possible.

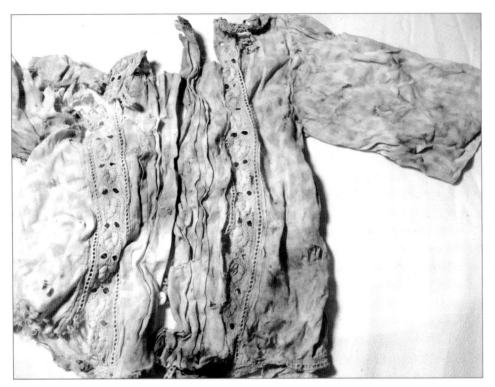

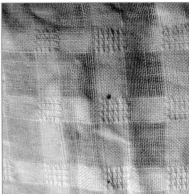

Baby gown from the late 1800s,
with close-ups of the fabric pattern
and lace work.

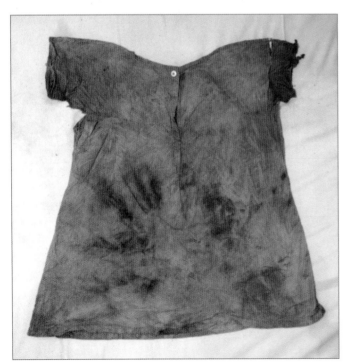

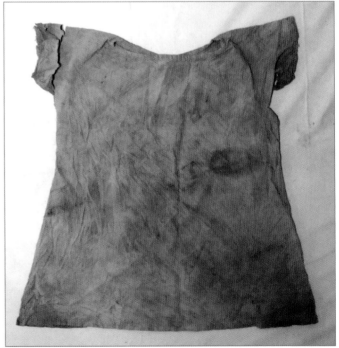

Little girl's dress from the 1870s; front and back.

Blue checkered jacket, ca. 1880s. The patching is newly basted-in pieces from a different patterned fabric of the period.

A jacket very similar to this was pictured in a 1902 Sears & Roebuck Co. catalogue.

169

Back of the ca. 1880s jacket. The "cut" of the shirt is simple and is not made to fit well.

Close-up of the cinch strap on the lower back of the jacket.

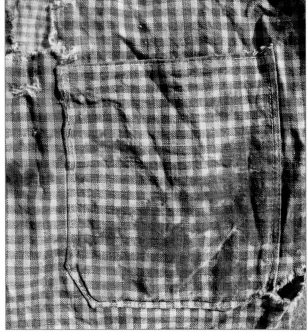

Breast pocket of ca. 1880s jacket.

Chinese-style shirt
from the late 1800s

Close-up of a fastener
on the Chinese-style
shirt.

Close-up of the
breast pocket.

Man's shirt from the late 1800s

Close-ups of the two types
of buttons on the shirt.

171

A pair of salesman's sample pants made by J. Wahl's of Chicago, Illinois, sometime between 1883 and 1890. They are small enough for a child to wear, but are proportioned like an adult pair of pants. I can tentatively date these by the fact that J. Wahl's patent was granted in 1883 and the pants are not riveted, which they would likely be if they were made after 1890—the expiration date of the rivet patent. (courtesy of Hitoshi Yamada)

Back of the J. Wahl sample pants.
(courtesy of Hitoshi Yamada)

Upper part of the J. Wahl sample pants showing the heavy stitching at the pocket corners. (courtesy of Hitoshi Yamada)

Upper right back of the J. Wahl sample pants. The pocket is unadorned, but it looks like it has a double thickness of material to strengthen the opening. Note the belt loop used for the patented waist adjustment. The belt loop was part of J. Wahl's patent and may have prevented the use of them by other pants makers until the patent expired in 1900 (which is about when belt loops came into general usage). (courtesy of Hitoshi Yamada)

Close-up of the label on J. Wahl's sample "Adjustable Pantaloon Overalls."(courtesy of Hitoshi Yamada)

(No Model.)

J. WAHL.
OVERALLS.

No. 275,441.   Patented Apr. 10, 1883.

Fig. 1.

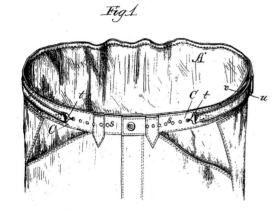

Fig. 2.

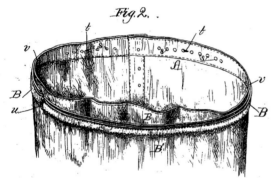

Witnesses:
C. C. Gaylord.
E. McCaffry

Inventor:
Joseph Wahl,
By P. C. Dyrenforth,
attorney.

Of note in this patent are two things: one—the patent illustration shows a strengthening design of a tab of extra material extending from the waistband to cover the pocket corner. This design is not included in the patent claims and could not be used in manufacture (I think this extra tab of material too closely resembles Samuel Krouse's 1875 patent). Two—this patent includes belt loops.

UNITED STATES PATENT OFFICE.

JOSEPH WAHL, OF CHICAGO, ILLINOIS.

OVERALLS.

SPECIFICATION forming part of Letters Patent No. 275,441, dated April 10, 1883.

Application filed February 7, 1883. (No model.)

To all whom it may concern:

Be it known that I, JOSEPH WAHL, a citizen of the United States, residing at Chicago, in the county of Cook and State of Illinois, have invented certain new and useful Improvements in Overalls; and I hereby declare the following to be a full, clear, and exact description of the same.

One of the chief difficulties encountered by manufacturers and dealers in supplying the trade with overalls is the great variety required in the matter of waist measurements, owing to the inadequacy of the means hitherto employed for graduating the size of the garment at that point. This difficulty not only works a disadvantage to the manufacturer by requiring him to provide a large number of different sizes, and to the dealer by requiring him to keep various sizes on hand, some of which may never be called for, but it is also a matter of much inconvenience to the ultimate purchaser, who often finds it impossible to obtain a properly-fitting garment without vexatious delay, and perhaps additional expense.

The object of my invention is to overcome the above difficulty by providing the garment with an adjusting device at the waist, of such scope as to admit of its being fitted to any waist, (provided of course that the latter be not too large for the garment to encompass,) and so easily operated as to give no trouble to the user.

To these ends my invention consists in providing a pantaloon garment with two straps, (which may be of the same fabric as the garment itself,) secured to the waist, one toward each side, with a view to being passed around the back, and one of the straps having a suitable opening in it for the passage through it of the other, and combining with these features means for attaching the straps to the front portion of the waist at the adjacent sides of the front opening, with a tension suited to the requirement.

It consists, also, in the particular construction which, for effectiveness and economy, I prefer to employ as to the waistband and straps, in combination with an adjustable fastening device at the front; and, also, in the particular construction which, for like reasons, I prefer to employ as to the adjustable fastening device at the front, in combination with the two straps attached to the waist and passing in contrary directions around the back, all as hereinafter more fully set forth.

In the accompanying drawings, Figure 1 is a front view, and Fig. 2 a rear view, of the upper portion of a pantaloon garment provided with my improvements.

A is the waist portion of the garment, and B B' the two straps, preferably secured thereto at about the points v, though these points may vary (especially by being brought farther around toward the rear) without affecting the general nature of the invention. The strap B' is provided with an opening, u, at a point within convenient reach of the wearer, for the passage of the strap B, which opening I prefer to form of an interposed wire link, as shown, though a transverse slit, like a button-hole, may be used instead, if desired. While any convenient method may be adopted for attaching these straps to the garment, the one represented in the drawings is recommended as, in my opinion, the simplest and most practical that can be devised. In this the waistband C, instead of extending entirely around the garment, as is generally the case, extends only across the front, being sewed thereto as far as the points v, and being continued into the straps B and B' from that point onward. This strengthens that part of the waist which alone is subjected to strain when in use. The back, which is relieved from all strain by the operation of the straps, is of only one thickness below the hem. The straps are of such length that when passed in contrary directions around the back to the front, with the waist of the garment fully distended, their ends will fall considerably short of the front opening, and here the straps and the upper margin of the garment are provided with means for attaching the two together, and at the same time allowing the tension of the straps to be graduated to any required degree, thus enlarging or contracting the garment at the waist, as circumstances may require. For the purpose of this adjustment, various contrivances might be adopted, all more or less effective. For example, the end of each strap might be provided with a button on the inside, and the front of the waist with a series of button-holes on each side of the front opening; or (though this is less desirable) each strap, toward its outer end,

---

2   275,441

might be provided with a series of button-holes, and the margin of the garment with a button on each side of the front opening, at some distance therefrom; but the way which I prefer, as the simplest, cheapest, and most effective of all, is to provide the end of each strap with a hook, t, and the front of the garment, at the upper margin, with a series of metal eyelets, s, on each side of the front opening, sufficient in number to admit of a considerable range in the adjustment of the garment, all as shown in the drawings. After putting on the garment the ends of the straps B and B' are brought around to the front, as represented in the drawings, and the hooks t inserted in such of the eyelets s as afford the required degree of tightness. This throws the strain partly upon the straps B and B' and partly upon the front, which latter, as before stated, is re-enforced by the band C. The back gathers together between the points v to conform to the person of the wearer, and thus sustains no strain.

From the foregoing description it will be obvious that with my improvements the number of different waist measurements in overalls may be reduced to two or three general sizes, while at the same time the convenience of the garment and comfort of the wearer are increased.

What I claim as new, and desire to secure by Letters Patent, is—

1. In a pantaloon garment, the straps B and B', secured to the waist toward the sides thereof, the strap B' having an opening, u, for the passage of the strap B when the two are passed in contrary directions around the back of the garment, as shown, in combination with means, substantially as described, for attaching each strap to the front of the waist at the adjacent side of the front opening, and for regulating the tension of the straps, as set forth.

2. In a pantaloon garment, the band C, sewed to the front margin of the waist, and terminating at or near the sides, and prolonged into straps B and B', the strap B' having an opening, u, for the passage of the strap B, in combination with means, substantially as described, for attaching each strap to the front of the waist at the adjacent side of the front opening, and for regulating the tension of the straps, as set forth.

3. In a pantaloon garment, the straps B and B', secured to the waist toward the sides thereof, the strap B' having an opening, u, for the passage of the strap B when the two are passed in contrary directions around the back of the garment, as shown, in combination with the hook t upon the ends of the straps, and the eyelets s on each side of the front opening, substantially as described.

JOSEPH WAHL.

In presence of—
WM. H. DYRENFORTH,
EPHRAIM BANNING.

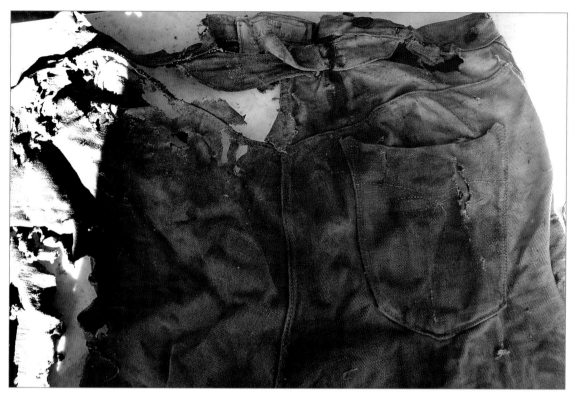

A pair of waist overalls from the 1880s. The heavy stitching at the pocket corners was a non-patent design that could be used by any maker. The lack of rivets very probably dates these to before 1890. (courtesy of Brit Eaton)

The cloth label only says "The Montana" and the size. No maker is given. Likely these were made on the East Coast. If they had been made on the West Coast, the label probably would have said that. (courtesy of Brit Eaton)

Detail of pattern on the 1860s or '70s apron.

Woman's apron from the the 1860s or '70s.

Close-up of the brim edge.

A floppy brim hat from the 1870s.

A pair of leather gloves used in a mine in the 1870s or 1880s. The owner must have been doing something that required him to use the ends of his fingers as both gloves have the fingertips worn off.

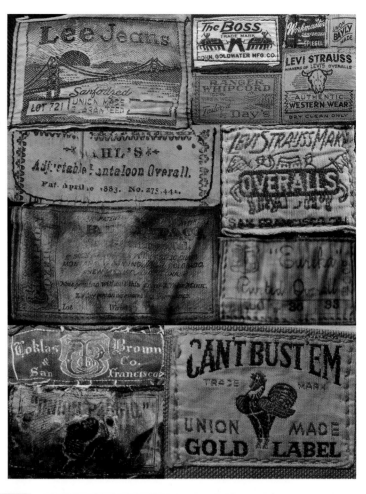

A montage of clothing labels from the late nineteenth and early twentieth centuries. Half of the garments bearing these labels are shown in previous chapters.

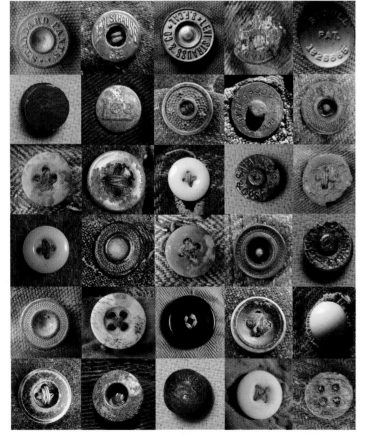

Three suspender buttons and an early Levi Strauss & Co. rivet (the inside part).

A montage of buttons and rivets from the late nineteenth and early twentieth centuries.

A montage of clothing fabrics from the 1870s and 1880s.

A third montage of clothing fabrics from the 1870s and 1880s.

Another montage of clothing fabrics from the 1870s and 1880s.

The last montage of clothing fabrics from the 1870s and 1880s.

Denim Manufacturing & Wear Patterns of Late Nineteenth Century Jeans

Denim was in use long before the 1870s, when *Levi Strauss & Co.* began making blue jeans under their patent for riveted work wear. In those days, denim was generally defined as heavy, coarse cotton twilled fabric. It was used for items other than clothing—such as carpet—but in clothing it was mainly used for overalls. The Civil War-era work pants shown in the chapter on pre-1873 jeans are made of denim.

I've only recently learned the rudiments of weaving and denim manufacturing. Without this knowledge, I found that I was missing a lot of information about the old jeans that crossed my desk. For my education, I've depended on the experts: Ralph Tharpe at *Cone Denim LLC* and the visual aids from Cotton, Inc. I will continue this section by giving a simplified description of the old weaving process beginning with the thread arrangement on the loom.

The warp threads—also called ends—are the ones tied to the loom and stretched out from it to frames called harnesses. Some of the warp threads are controlled by one harness and others by another harness. There can be several harnesses depending on the weave pattern desired. These harnesses move up or down depending on the weave pattern that's set. For denim, these warp threads are dyed indigo. The weft thread or threads—also called fill or picks—are inserted back and forth through the warp threads to form the fabric. In denim, the weft threads are not dyed. The pattern of weaving is set by the movement of the harnesses that control which warp threads are over or under the weft thread as it passes between them.

Usually the pre-1873 work pants were made of lightweight denim, woven in a 2 x 1 pattern. What I believe to be the earliest pairs of Levi Strauss & Co. denim waist overalls were made of this lightweight denim. But, probably, within a few months after starting production, Levi Strauss & Co. began using heavier 3 x 1 denim. Both the 2 x 1 and 3 x 1 weave patterns have a "twill" or an apparent diagonal line on the surface of the fabric.

Other than the usual indigo blue color, denim differed from duck, the other common work pants material, in the way it was woven. The duck—also coarse cotton—was usually made in a plain 2 x 2 weave pattern. There is no "twill," or diagonal lines in this fabric.

I assume that these weave patterns were chosen for denim because they show more dyed threads on one side. This would save on indigo dye and the cost of the dying process since only half of the thread would have to be dyed. The indigo used was an all natural vegetable dye until about 1897 when synthetic indigo came on the market.

The 2 x 1 weave pattern was made by weaving the white, undyed weft thread over one blue warp thread and under two, repeating across the width of the loom. In the next row, the pattern was shifted one thread. This shifting gave the material the diagonal line or "twill." For the 3 x 1 weave pattern, the undyed weft thread passes over one dyed thread and under three dyed threads, showing even more blue thread on one side than the other. The 2 x 2 filling rib weave pattern used for duck was made by passing the weft thread over two warp threads and under two. The next row would repeat this pattern, and then the next two rows would be the inverse. This would give a "square" pattern to the material with no diagonal "twill" lines.

I've often referred to denim or duck pants in earlier chapters as being made of "heavy" or "light" material. In the 1800s, fabric weights were measured in ounces per running yard of material. For instance, in an 1879 catalogue, *Levi Strauss & Co.* referred to their duck pants and vests as "10 oz." However, this is not a direct equivalent to a 10 oz. duck weight today. Two things make a modern weight measurement less than what was given in the late 1800s. First, the looms used to make duck and denim for work pants in the late 1800s were 28 inches wide; so, a running yard of material was 8 inches less than a yard wide. This would make the 10 oz. duck used by *Levi Strauss & Co.* equivalent to almost 13 ounces by today's measure. Second, duck and denim were not washed after weaving, but used directly off the loom. The shrinkage from washing the modern fabric adds more weight per square yard—making the final equivalent duck material about 14 ounces per square yard. Nine oz. denim of 1880 would be equivalent to about 13 oz modern preshrunk denim.

Fabric weights were controlled by the packing of the threads and, mainly, by the size of the thread.

Denim made with in the 3 x 1 weave pattern was almost always heavier than denim made with the 2 x 1 pattern because the 3 x 1 pattern could accommodate heavier yarn, and heavier yarn would make the jeans sturdier. The 2 x 1 pattern was used when sturdiness was not as important as cutting the cost of manufacturing. The 2 x 1 weave could make cloth made from thinner, lighter yarn appear substantial. But, if heavy yarn was used in the 2 x 1 pattern, the denim would be too stiff.

It is reported that, from the beginning, *Levi Strauss & Co.* used denim made by the *Amoskeag Manufacturing Company* in New Hampshire for making riveted work pants in San Francisco. But, the very earliest riveted work pants that I believe were made by *Levi Strauss & Co.* are of lightweight 2 x 1 denim. So, that denim may have been manufactured elsewhere. Regardless, all denim used by *Levi Strauss & Co.* from then until 1915 came from the 28-inch looms of Amoskeag. In 1915, *Cone Mills* of Greensboro, North Carolina, began supplying some of the denim for *Levi Strauss & Co.* By 1922, *Cone Mills* took over as the sole supplier.

I assume that the North Carolina company had the advantage of being closer to the source of cotton and that the power source for Amoskeag, the Merrimack River, was no longer an advantage in an age of machine power. In 1923, one year after gaining the exclusive business of *Levi Strauss & Co.*, Cone Mills claimed to be the largest denim manufacturer in the world. *Cone Mills* also used 28-inch looms, which provided a sufficient amount of selvedge (edge) to make the selvedge-seam pants of *Levi Strauss & Co.* When used at the long side seam of work pants, this selvedge would prevent raveling of the fabric edge. *Cone Mills*—now *Cone Denim LLC*—still has some of those 28-inch looms; but most of them were destroyed long ago.

I have only mentioned the source for the denim and duck used by *Levi Strauss & Co.* because I know nothing about the source of the fabrics used by the other competing work pants manufacturers in San Francisco during the 1870s and 1880s. Since the records for the other pants makers in San Francisco were all destroyed by the fires following the 1906 earthquake, that information will have to come from somewhere else—perhaps in the records of the old denim mills back East.

By examining a pair of denim and duck pants you can tell a lot about how and in what type of conditions the pants were used by the wear patterns found on the surface of the pants. Miners and mill workers wore heavy duck and denim to protect their skin from the harsh conditions of the workplace, whether working with ore or working in a mill with acids. Denim and duck were essential extra layers of protection that other trousers could not provide.

When studying a pair of old work pants, the marks, rips, stains, and fade patterns can give us clues as to how the wearer lived and worked. Miners that worked in dark conditions in the 1870s or 1880s will have candle wax droplets on the front of their pants legs. Mill workers in those times often have acid holes and, from my experience, a 4-6" vertical rip in the fabric on the upper part of the left (the wearer's left) leg. I have seen a rip like this on at least four pairs, as well as a large hole, on the front left leg. Repetitive motion and leaning in on a piece of machinery I assume would be the cause of these rips that show up in the same area of these pants. Candle wax rarely shows up on mill workers' pants. I assume this is due to the access to sunlight in the workplace and because the workers left their work pants in changing rooms. They would use candles at home with their own garments.

Duck and denim were not only used as clothing, but as tools for the miners as well. Supplies were scarce in the West at that time, so they would reuse the materials at hand. Miners would cut the denim, duck, and canvas to create long, wide strips that they would apply homemade glue to and wrap the air pipe connections/joints that traversed the length of many mines. They would then usually wrap twine around the joint for added strength. Denim has been found plugging holes on machinery and insulating areas around mine doors. Clothing has also been found in attics and floors of houses to insulate the house from the elements.

There also have been natural processes at work for the past 130 to 140 years that each garment has endured. I am sure that most items have perished in the West and the clues that they may have provided as to the designs and the wearers' lives perished with them. But the few examples that remain, and those yet to be found, provide clues about the conditions they have been in since the wearers tossed them out. Typically, any pieces of clothing found above ground in shelter will have damage from rats and mice, but will usually have intact metal components that have not rusted. Any clothing that has recently been unearthed from a natural process such as a flood will have sun damage and bleaching on any exposed surfaces. Clothing that has been found below ground will typically have its metal pieces rusted and corroded, the extent of which depends on the acidity of the ground.

Denim, to my knowledge, is one of the most functional, useful items one can wear when working in rough conditions. Denim allows your skin to breath and is more comfortable than wool or leather. The following images are examples of various wear patterns I have seen.

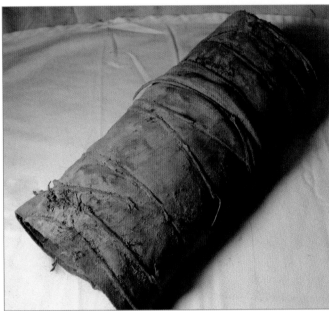

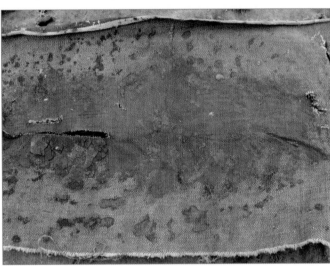

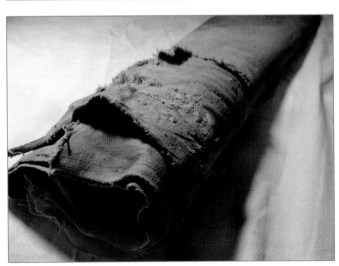

From top to bottom: a duck pant leg piece used to wrap an air pipe. There are cord marks on the fabric surface where it was tied on. Next, a denim pant leg strip used to wrap a pipe. Note the numerous rust stains and the glue remains in the middle of the strip. And last, a strongly twilled denim pant leg piece used as pipe wrapping. Note again the rust stains and the caked remains of sealant.

This piece of duck pant leg was reused as air pipe wrapping to seal a joint.

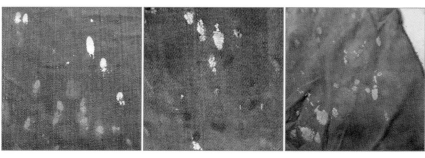

Pant legs pieces showing use in mines. The first two are denim and the last is duck. All three have candle wax drippings on them. Note the very white color of the wax drippings. The drippings are quite hard and brittle.

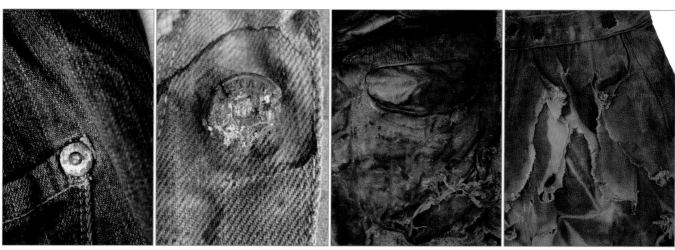

A grouping of pants parts showing different natural weathering patterns. The denim pants on the far left were buried for about one hundred years and are very stained by dirt and the copper rivets are corroded. The next is a close-up of a suspender button on a pair of denim pants that were buried in an acidic environment. The steel is nearly rusted away. The next denim pants rear pocket area shows sun bleaching from partial exposure. The far right pair of pants has extensive damage from exposure, including a missing leg. All are from pants shown in previous chapters.

Three pair of denim overalls showing work wear. The one on the left has rips and holes typical if millwork wear. The middle pair has a wear hole from carrying something in the front pocket. The one on the right has extensive surface wear perhaps from leaning against machinery in a mill.

Patching on denim overalls done during the original useful life of the pants. The far left patch is a crudely executed, small inside patch using another type of denim. The next is a large outside patch over a wear area using the same denim type. The next is a very large leg patch that seems to be made to carry things (high grading?). The top of the patch shows indications of once being stitched, but it also shows signs of pocket-top wear. There is no hole underneath the patch. The far right pair has a leg patch over a wear hole and the patch shows wear in the same place.

Late 1800s Items From the Old West

These additional items were included to provide inspirational images to the reader and to create a more complete picture of how people of the late 1800s lived in the West.

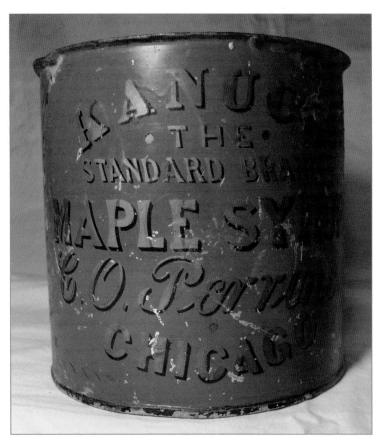

Quart-size maple syrup can from the 1870s. The well-worn appearance of the can is because it was used in a mine to carry oil.

The hand-stenciled wording on the top of the maple syrup can is cautioning the user against something that I haven't taken the time to decipher. Being a good speller must not have been a requirement of the stencilers job.

A hand-blown whiskey bottle from the early 1870s. Men in the mining camps drank prodigious amounts of spirits and preferred bourbon from Kentucky.

An assortment of bottles from the late 1800s. These range in age from the 1860s to the 1890s. All were hand-blown in glass factories in the Eastern U.S. and in San Francisco. The older bottles, and especially those from San Francisco, are cruder. Most pictured contained medicine or spirits, but in the front are an inkbottle and a spice bottle.

A toothpick card cologne bottle, often suspected of being secondarily used for opium, which was legal then.

The greenish bottles in the left background were used for medicines. The greenish color comes from iron impurities in the sand used to make the glass. In the front left is an inkbottle next to a cobalt blue perfume bottle. The little faceted glass dish in the front is a 'salt cellar' used to dispense salt at the dinner table.

From left to right, in the foreground, is a Jamaica Ginger (nasty stuff I hear), a large beer bottle (ubiquitous in mining camps of the Old West), a shoe polish bottle, two clear medicinal bottles, and on the far right, a soda bottle made in San Francisco.

Federal revenue stamp on a chewing tobacco plug package.

Chewing tobacco plug package sticker.

Label on an 1870s chewing tobacco plug package.

A maple syrup can marketed by a West Coast firm (Pacific Coast Syrup Co.)

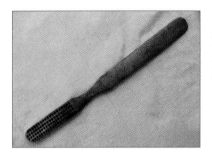

A toothbrush from the late 1800s. The handle is made of bone and it probably had horsehair bristles.

A quilt blanket from an 1870s mining camp.

Playing cards from the 1870s. There were no numerals on them; they had to count the "pips."

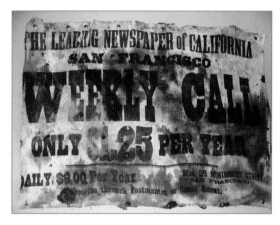

Advertising banner for the *San Francisco Call* newspaper from the 1870s. The newspaper offices were destroyed in the fires started by the 1906 earthquake.

An ore sack used in the 1870s for silver ore that was destined for a mill—front and back.

The partial end of a candle box. It was reused as a wedge.

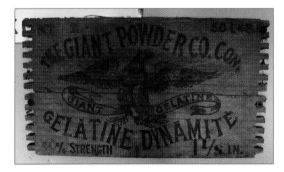

The end piece of a dynamite box from the late nineteenth century. It held 50 sticks.

The side of an evaporated cream box used for another purpose in a mine (the white spots on it are candle wax drippings). Highland Brand Evaporated Cream was the first evaporated milk produced. It was first sold in 1885.

Duluth Pack Sack used to carry goods on a man's back by tumpline or shoulder straps. It was made in Duluth, Minnesota, by Camille Poirer, a French-Canadian who filed for a patent on it in 1882. (courtesy of Mike Hodis)

Close-up of one of the "pack sack" buckles. (courtesy of Mike Hodis)

Front and back of the "pack sack." (courtesy of Mike Hodis)

Civil War-era canvas tent made in Sacramento, California, by Weinstock & Lubin.

188

Brand name on the side of a leather boot piece from the late 1800s.

Square nails pre-1880.

Cinch-strap buckle on long underwear, ca 1870s.

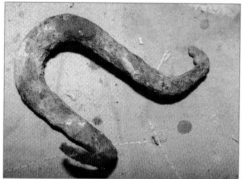

Leather work boot piece from the late 1800s, with a square nail in it.

Old rusted tin can, ca 1870s.

189

Conclusion

To the best of my knowledge, this is the first time that the story of the early development of jeans in the Old West has been put together. The commerce war between riveted (*Levi Strauss & Co.*) and non-riveted jeans lasted from 1873 to 1890. And this struggle between Levi Strauss and the other work pants wholesalers of San Francisco has only now come to light. As stated before, all of the records and remains of that period were destroyed in the fire following the 1906 San Francisco earthquake, leaving a void in history that I have only recently, sketchily, pieced together.

Only after years of discussions with colleagues, hours of examining examples of old jeans and fragments, and, finally, research into the sparse records, was I able to form the picture given in this book. I have been lucky enough to have access to remaining pants, as I have found that they are exceedingly rare; although, there may very well be more that have gone unrecognized.

Of course, some or a lot of what I have written herein is still theory – the best ideas that fit what few facts are available. The story is not yet complete. There is very likely much more information out there in libraries, archives, photo collections, private collections, and family histories. But, the time has come to put what I know on paper.

I love old denim, old jeans, old clothes, and the Old West. My passion for these things makes me want to share what I have learned with others.

There is, admittedly, little glamour in old discarded work pants – they are often no more than dirty cloth fragments barely recognizable as jeans. But, because of their connection to our modern society, with its near-obsession with jeans, they have historical importance. There is no break in the link between the jeans made in San Francisco in the 1870s and 1880s and the jeans being made today. Photographs of miners and mill workers from that time show them in pants that are nearly identical with the jeans I wear. But, today there has been a marked expansion in their use to include not only work wear, but also everyday wear and, at times, quasi-formal wear. To wit: my father-in-law was in Sofia, Bulgaria, shortly after the fall of communism there, and was invited to attend the ballet at the National Theater. When he asked what he should wear, he was told that the proper attire was blue jeans.

In the Old West, blue jeans were one of a workingman's tools. They protected his lower body, they carried items of use, and they were comfortable enough to wear all day long. And, with the invention of the riveted jeans, they were sturdy enough to last for years. They often found other uses, also. I have seen tar-soaked blue jean scraps wrapped around air pipes at old mills. I surmise that this is why some of the old, discarded jeans I have seen have had their legs cut off.

To me, old San Francisco-made blue jeans have functional beauty – like old steam engines with all of the pipes and workings on the outside. Not only the riveted jeans of *Levi Strauss & Co.*, but also, and perhaps more so, the non-riveted jeans with strengthening features sewn on the outside, like the designs of *B. & O. Greenebaum*, *A. B. Elfelt*, and *S. R. Krause*.

Although this book is primarily about the jeans manufacturing companies in San Francisco during the late 1800s, there were a large number of independent tailors working in San Francisco at the time who made clothes-to-fit. Work pants could be bought ready-made off the shelves of dry goods stores in all of the Western towns and mining camps of the period, but dress clothes were probably mostly purchased from these independent tailors.

Remember that the first riveted denim jeans were made by Jacob Davis in his tailor shop in Reno, Nevada. In fact, his inclusion of a watch pocket on work pants may have stemmed from his familiarity with making suit pants, which customarily came with one. Also, Jacob's addition of a back pocket to his work pants, something not normally found on work pants of the period, but often on dress pants, suggests that he used a dress pants pattern for his work pants design. So, the modern form of jeans, with a watch pocket and back pockets, probably owes its existence to the melding of features from dress pants with work pants by a tailor.

Like many relics of the Old West, old jeans have monetary value. Pre-1890 pairs of jeans made by *Levi Strauss & Co.* have sold for nearly $50,000. The non-riveted jeans made by the competitors of *Levi Strauss & Co.* have significant value also. But, estimating that value is more difficult because their sales are generally not announced. They are very rare, but until now their place in history has, probably, not been understood.

190

The Bay of San Francisco, the Metropolis of the Pacific Coast and its Suburban Cities, a History, vol. II. 1892. Chicago, Illinois: Lewis Publishing Company, p. 416 and 417.

Bishop's Oakland Directory. 1877-8. San Francisco, California: B. C. Vandall.

Bishop's Oakland Directory. 1879-80. San Francisco, California: Directory Publishing Company.

The Builders of a Great City, San Francisco's Representative Men, the City, its History and Commerce, Vol. 1. 1891. San Francisco, California: San Francisco Journal of Commerce Publishing Co.

The City of San Francisco and the State of California. 1892. San Francisco, California: Metropolitan Publishing Co.

Cogan, S. G., compiler. 1973. *The Jews of San Francisco and the Greater Bay Area, 1849-1919.* Berkeley, California: Western Jewish History Center, Judah L. Magnes Memorial Museum.

Coronet Magazine. June 1956.

Cotton Incorporated. 2006. *The Art of Denim Manufacturing.* Cary, North Carolina. www.cottoninc.com

Cray, Ed. 1978. *Levi's.* Boston, Massachusetts: Houghton Mifflin Company.

Crocker-Langley's San Francisco City Directory. 1863. San Francisco, California.

Daily Alta California, 27 April 1878, 5 July 1884, and 7 July 1889. San Francisco, California.

A Directory of the City of Oakland and the Town of Alameda. 1874. San Francisco, California: Henry G. Langley.

Directory of the Township and City of Oakland. 1869. California: B. F. Stillwell.

Fifty Years of Odd Fellowship in California. 1899. H. S. San Francisco, California: Crocker Company.

Glanz, Rudolf. April 1954. "Jews and Chinese in America." *Jewish Social Studies, a quarterly journal devoted to contemporary and historical aspects of Jewish life.* XVI (2): 219-234.

Great Register of Voters. 1880. San Francisco, California.

Greenebaum family narrative, unpublished. 1914. Berkeley, California: Western Jewish History Center.

The Hebrew. Friday, February 9, 1872. San Francisco, California.

Hittel, John, S. 1882. *Commerce and Industry of the Pacific Coast of North America.* San Francisco, California: A. L. Bancroft and Co.

Invoice of Steinhart Brothers. 1865. Berkeley, California: Western Jewish History Center.

Kahn, A. F. 2002. *Jewish Voices of the California Gold Rush, a Documentary History, 1849-1880.* Detroit, Michigan: Wayne State University Press.

Langley's San Francisco Directory, 1862, 1864, 1865, 1867-1869, 1871-1889. San Francisco, California.

Langley's San Francisco Directory, 1889, 1890. W.H.L. San Francisco, California: Corran.

Marsh, Graham and Paul Trynka. 2002. *Denim, From Cowboys to Catwalks: a History of the World's Most Legendary Fabric.* United Kingdom: Aurum Press.

Mear's Sacramento Directory, 1861 and 1862.

Meyer, Martin A. 1916. *Western Jewry, an Account of the Achievements of the Jews and Judaism in California Including Eulogies and Bibliographies.* San Francisco, California: Emanu-El.

Narell, Irena. 1981. *Our City, the Jews of San Francisco.* San Diego, California: Howell North Publishers, Inc.

Partnership agreements between A. B. Elfelt and A. L. Levi, 1867 and 1884. Photocopies. Berkeley, California: Western Jewish History Center.

The Portland Directory. 1863. S. J. McCormick.

Rafael, R. K. 1987. *Western Jewish History Center, Guide to Archival and Oral History Collections.* Berkeley, California: Western Jewish History Center, Judah L. Magnes Memorial Museum.

Rochlin, Harriet and Fred. 1984. *Pioneer Jews, a New Life in the Far West.* New York, New York: Houghton Mifflin Company.

Roth, Art. Fall 1952. "The Levi's Story, a Standard Texan Garment Has Become an American Institution." *American Heritage Magazine.* 49-51.

The Sacramento Directory. 1861 and 1862. H. J. Bidleman, Compiler. John J. Murphy, Publisher.

The Sacramento Directory. 1877-8. San Francisco, California: B. C. Vandall.

The San Francisco Directory. 1861. San Francisco, California: Henry G. Langley.

San Francisco, Her Great Manufacturing, Commercial and Financial Institutions Are Famed the World Over, 1904-1905. San Francisco, California: The Pacific Art Company.

Sullivan, James. 2006. *Jeans, a Cultural History of an American Icon.* New York, New York: Gotham Books.